MOSES

VOL. III

GREAT LEADER AND LAWGIVER

by Theodore H. Epp
Director
Back to the Bible Broadcast

A
BACK TO THE BIBLE
PUBLICATION

$1.50

Back to the Bible
Lincoln, Nebraska 68501

85,000 printed to date—1976
(5-4906—85M—16)
ISBN 0-8474-1237-7

Printed in the United States of America

Contents

Chapter 1

Israel Becomes a Nation

By the end of the time of plagues which God brought on Egypt, Moses was established beyond any doubt, both before Egypt and before Israel, as God's man for the great task of leading the Israelites.

The Bible says, "Moreover the man Moses was very great in the land of Egypt, in the sight of Pharaoh's servants, and in the sight of the people" (Ex. 11:3). After the Israelites had been delivered from the Egyptians, the Bible records: "Israel saw that great work which the Lord did upon the Egyptians: and the people feared the Lord, and believed the Lord, and his servant Moses" (14:31).

Only as Moses' leadership was fully established with Israel was he able to proceed in leading them out of Egypt, through the desert and to the land of his fathers.

From Exodus 12:40,41 we learn that the Israelites had been in Egypt for 430 years: "Now the sojourning of the children of Israel, who dwelt in Egypt, was four hundred and thirty years. And it came to pass at the end of the four hundred and thirty years, even the selfsame day it came to pass, that all the hosts of the Lord went out from the land of Egypt."

God's Promises to Abraham

God's program for the people of Israel actually began with His call of Abraham, who was then known as Abram. God's call and promise of blessings on Abraham and his descendants are recorded in Genesis 12:1-3: "Now the Lord had said unto Abram, Get thee out of thy country, and from

5

thy kindred, and from thy father's house, unto a land that I will shew thee: and I will make of thee a great nation, and I will bless thee, and make thy name great; and thou shalt be a blessing: and I will bless them that bless thee, and curse him that curseth thee: and in thee shall all families of the earth be blessed." Note especially the words "I will make of thee a great nation."

God's promise to Abraham was confirmed to Abraham's son Isaac. God told Isaac, "Sojourn in this land, and I will be with thee, and will bless thee; for unto thee, and unto thy seed, I will give all these countries, and I will perform the oath which I sware unto Abraham thy father; and I will make thy seed to multiply as the stars of heaven, and will give unto thy seed all these countries; and in thy seed shall all the nations of the earth be blessed; because that Abraham obeyed my voice, and kept my charge, my commandments, my statutes, and my laws" (26:3-5). Note especially the words "I will perform the oath which I sware unto Abraham thy father" (v. 3).

God's promise to Abraham was confirmed again to Jacob in a dream: "And, behold, the Lord stood above it [the ladder], and said, I am the Lord God of Abraham thy father, and the God of Isaac: the land whereon thou liest, to thee will I give it, and to thy seed; and thy seed shall be as the dust of the earth, and thou shalt spread abroad to the west, and to the east, and to the north, and to the south: and in thee and in thy seed shall all the families of the earth be blessed" (28:13,14).

Genesis 35:9-12 also confirmed to Jacob the promises God had made to Abraham: "And God appeared unto Jacob again, when he came out of Padan-aram, and blessed him. And God said unto him, Thy name is Jacob: thy name shall not be called any more Jacob, but Israel shall be thy name: and he called his name Israel. And God said unto him, I am God Almighty: be fruitful and multiply; a nation and a company of nations shall be of thee, and kings shall come out of thy loins; and the land which I gave Abraham and Isaac, to thee I will give it, and to thy seed after thee will I give the land." Verse 11 is especially significant: "God said unto him, I am God Almighty: be fruitful and multiply; a nation and a company of nations shall be of thee, and kings shall come out of thy loins."

Near the end of Jacob's life there was a famine in the land of Canaan, and food was available only in Egypt. The Bible records how Jacob's sons went down to Egypt and acquired food from their brother Joseph, although they were unaware at first of Joseph's identity. Later, Joseph disclosed his identity to his brothers and arranged to bring Jacob and the rest of the family to Egypt.

Although Jacob had looked forward to seeing his beloved son Joseph again, he was reluctant to leave the land of Canaan. However, God assured Jacob that he should go to Egypt and reiterated the Abrahamic covenant to him. God told Jacob, "I am God, the God of thy father: fear not to go down into Egypt; for I will there make of thee a great nation: I will go down with thee into Egypt; and I will also surely bring thee up again" (46:3,4). Notice that God planned to make a great nation of Jacob and his descendants in Egypt.

This fact is also evident from Deuteronomy 26:5, which records the words of Moses concerning his ancestor Jacob: "A Syrian ready to perish was my father, and he went down into Egypt, and sojourned there with a few, and became there a nation, great, mighty, and populous." Notice again the words "became there a nation."

Israel's Independence Day

So the Scriptures indicate that the descendants of Abraham actually became a nation while they were in Egypt. Before this time they were not known as a nation. A common expression concerning God's chosen people before this time was "children of Israel." This expression is derived from the fact that Jacob's name was changed to "Israel," for the angel of the Lord told him, "Thy name shall be called no more Jacob, but Israel: for as a prince hast thou power with God and with men, and hast prevailed" (Gen. 32:28).

Following this time, Jacob is commonly referred to as "Israel" and his descendants are referred to as the "children of Israel." The Book of Exodus uses the expression "children of Israel" several times in the first chapter (vv. 1,7,9,13). The 12 sons of Jacob were designated by the expression "children of Israel," and the 12 sons were destined to become the heads of the 12 tribes of Israel.

Before the Israelites were delivered from Egypt, God also referred to them as "my people," and through Moses he told Pharaoh, "Let my people go" (Ex. 5:1). But even though the descendants of Jacob were known as the "children of Israel" or "my people," they were not known as the "nation" of Israel. They became a nation on the day they left Egypt, so the day of the Exodus was truly an independence day for them.

That the time of the Exodus was also the time of the birth of Israel as a nation is evident from what God told Moses and Aaron in the land of Egypt: "This month shall be unto you the beginning of months: it shall be the first month of the year to you. Speak ye unto all the congregation of Israel, saying, In the tenth day of this month they shall take to them every man a lamb, according to the house of their fathers, a lamb for an house" (12:2,3). This was actually a fulfillment of what God had told Jacob: "Fear not to go down into Egypt; for I will there make of thee a great nation" (Gen. 46:3). The words of Exodus 12:2,3 tell of the time referred to in Deuteronomy 26:5 which says that Jacob "became there [in Egypt] a nation, great, mighty, and populous."

The month referred to in Exodus 12:2,3 is the month of April, known to the nation of Israel as "Abib." From that point on Israel was to keep the Feast of the Passover during this month. Deuteronomy 16:1 refers to this: "Observe the month of Abib, and keep the passover unto the Lord thy God: for in the month of Abib the Lord thy God brought thee forth out of Egypt by night." The Feast of the Passover was a remembrance of the beginning of the nation of Israel. As such, the Passover reminded the Israelites of everything that was foundational to the nation itself.

Just as the Israelites needed to be reminded of their beginning as a nation, those of us who know Jesus Christ as Saviour need to be reminded of the deliverance we have experienced. Colossians 1:12-14 refers to this deliverance: "Giving thanks unto the Father, . . . who hath delivered us from the power of darkness, and hath translated us into the kingdom of his dear Son: in whom we have redemption through his blood, even the forgiveness of sins."

Israel's redemption from Egypt constituted the first step in the life of the nation. The people stepped into freedom! Before that time they had been merely a group of slaves, but then they became a free nation. God redeemed them by blood and by His power.

Important Time Divisions

There are at least three important divisions in time. The first one occurred when Israel became a nation, which is the subject being considered in Exodus 12. At this time, God interrupted the ordinary course of the peoples' existence, and their previous history was disregarded; from this time forth they were known as a nation. The redemption of Israel constituted a new step in the nation's life.

A second important division in time occurred when the Lord Jesus Christ entered this world through the nation of Israel. The birth of Christ changed the marking of calendars; the chronology of the civilized world is dated from this time.

A third important division in time occurs when an individual trusts Jesus Christ as his personal Saviour. Although the popular expression says that life begins at 40, for the Christian, life begins at Calvary. Every member of the human race is born into this world dead in trespasses and sins (Eph. 2:1-6). Because of the sin nature that each person possesses, all are separated—or alienated—from God (4:18). But when a person receives Jesus Christ as personal Saviour, he becomes a "new creature: old things are passed away; behold, all things are become new" (II Cor. 5:17). The new birth marks the beginning of a new life.

Just as the past of the individual Israelites was disregarded, as far as national history was concerned, after they became a nation, so also the past life of an individual is disregarded by God when that person trusts Christ as Saviour. His spiritual life begins at that moment. This life is available by trusting in Christ as Saviour, for at that time a person experiences a spiritual birth. The Bible says, "Except a man be born again, he cannot see the kingdom of God" (John 3:3). The Bible also says, "He that hath the Son hath life; and he that hath not the Son of God hath not life" (I John 5:12).

Israel's Journey in Three Stages

Israel's journey from Egypt to Canaan occurred in three distinct stages. All three stages are outlined in Exodus 6:6-8.

The first stage is seen in verse 6. God said, "I will bring you out from under the burdens of the Egyptians, and I will rid you out of their bondage, and I will redeem you with a stretched out arm, and with great judgments."

The second stage is seen in verse 7, where God said, "I will take you to me for a people, and I will be to you a God."

The third stage is expressed in verse 8 in which God said, "I will bring you in unto the land, . . . I will give it you for an heritage."

Illustration of the Believer's Life

These three stages in Israel's journey from Egypt to Canaan also illustrate three stages in the individual believer's life today. The New Testament says, "Now these things happened to them as an example, and they were written for our instruction" (I Cor. 10:11, NASB).

Each believer should ask himself, In which one of these stages am I spiritually? Israel in Egypt is symbolic of the believer's being occupied with the things of the world. Israel in the desert is symbolic of the believer's being occupied with the self-life. During this time Israel grumbled and complained against Moses and against God, even though God was performing miracles to take care of them. God had to have much longsuffering and mercy toward Israel at this time. Israel in Canaan symbolizes the believer's being occupied with the things of God or the God-life. So if you know Jesus

Christ as Saviour, in what stage is your spiritual life? Are you concerned about the world, about self or about God?

The one who has trusted Jesus Christ as Saviour can be occupied with the things of the world so that he is in bondage just as the children of Israel were in bondage under the Egyptians. Such a believer is a slave to the world.

A believer who is occupied with self is self-centered and expends his energy for selfish delights. Perhaps he would not do the things the world does, but what he does is to satisfy his own selfish desires.

The believer who is occupied with Christ is experiencing the abundant life. Jesus said, "I am come that they might have life, and that they might have it more abundantly" (John 10:10). If the believer is to have an overcoming life, he must recognize the truth of Ephesians 6:12: "For we wrestle not against flesh and blood, but against principalities, against powers, against the rulers of the darkness of this world, against spiritual wickedness in high places." To do spiritual warfare, the believer must be in fellowship with the Lord through the Word and much prayer (Eph. 6:17,18). Only then can he overcome evil.

God's plan for Israel included total deliverance. The Lord promised to deliver Israel from condemnation, from burdens and from bondage. God said, "I will bring you out from under the burdens of the Egyptians, and I will rid you out of their bondage, and I will redeem you with a stretched out arm, and with great judgments" (Ex. 16:6). The Passover and deliverance through the Red Sea accomplished all of these for the Israelites. This was deliverance from the world.

God promised to be with the Israelites in their desert experience and to take them to Himself: "I will take you to me for a people, and I will be to you a God: and ye shall know that I am the Lord your God, which bringeth you out from under the burdens of the Egyptians" (v. 7). At this point, the Israelites were not ready for the warfare they would encounter in the land. God used the desert experience to prepare them for this warfare.

The people of Canaan heard how God delivered the Israelites from the Egyptians, and as a result they feared the Israelites. However, the Israelites themselves were not spiritually strong enough to conquer as God wanted them to conquer. He had to take time to train them out in the desert. They needed to be delivered from the self-life.

Having been delivered from the world and from self, Israel needed to be delivered to God for true warfare and rest in the land. God promised this to them in Exodus 6:8: "And I will bring you in unto the land, concerning the which I did swear to give it to Abraham, to Isaac, and to Jacob; and I will give it you for an heritage: I am the Lord." It was not enough that God had promised the land to the Israelites. First they had to enter the land and then conquer it. Finally, as they believed God, they were to follow through and take possession of the land He had promised to them. This was spiritual warfare and involved being occupied with the things of God and especially with God Himself.

God Works for the Believer

God has a similar plan, or program, for the believer. First, the believer is delivered from the guilt and condemnation of sin by the redemptive work of Jesus Christ. This is altogether God's work through Christ in behalf of the believer. It is something God has done for us; it is not something we do ourselves. It is totally the work of God. Ephesians 1:7 speaks of this work of God for us: "In whom we have redemption through his blood, the forgiveness of sins, according to the riches of his grace." Ephesians 2:5 says, "Even when we were dead in sins, [he] hath quickened us [made us alive] together with Christ, (by grace ye are saved)."

The Book of Romans has much to say about the deliverance of the believer from the guilt and condemnation of sin. "Being justified freely by his grace through the redemption that is in Christ Jesus" (3:24). "But God commendeth his love toward us, in that, while we were yet sinners, Christ died for us. Much more then, being now justified by his blood, we shall be saved from wrath through him. For if, when we were enemies, we were reconciled to God by the death of his Son, much more, being reconciled, we shall be saved by his life" (5:8-10).

So first of all, as believers we have been taken from the world, where we were condemned. But God has also made provisions for us to be released from the slavery and bondage of sin. This is what Romans 6 is all about. Notice especially verses 3-6: "Know ye not, that so many of us as were baptized into Jesus Christ were baptized into his death? Therefore we are buried with him by baptism into death: that like as Christ was raised up from the dead by the glory of the Father, even so we also should walk in newness of life. For if we have been planted together in the likeness of his death, we shall be also in the likeness of his resurrection: knowing this, that our old man is [literally, was] crucified with him, that the body of sin might be destroyed, that henceforth we should not serve sin."

This is all God's doing, and it is all part of the first step that has been accomplished *for* us through the Lord Jesus Christ. All of this is made effective for us by the work of the Holy Spirit, producing life in us. His life-giving ministry is mentioned in John 3:5,6: "Jesus answered, Verily, verily, I say unto thee, Except a man be born of water and of the Spirit, he cannot enter into the kingdom of God. That which is born of the flesh is flesh; and that which is born of the Spirit is spirit."

So the first stage of the believer's life with the Lord is redemption from the guilt, condemnation, power and slavery of sin. If you have trusted Jesus Christ as your personal Saviour, this has been accomplished in your behalf. You need to thank God for this and live accordingly.

God Works in the Believer

The second stage of the believer's life with the Lord is deliverance from the weakness of the self-life and training for usefulness for God. This training is accomplished by Christ's work *in* us. The Scriptures emphasize more what Christ does in us than what He does through us.

In this regard, note the following verses: "Being confident of this very thing, that he which hath begun a good work in you will perform it until the day of Jesus Christ" (Phil. 1:6).

"According as he hath chosen us in him before the foundation of the world, that we should be holy and without blame before him in love: having predestinated us unto the adoption of children by Jesus Christ to himself, according to the good pleasure of his will, to the praise of the glory of his grace, wherein he hath made us accepted in the beloved" (Eph. 1:4-6).

"Hope maketh not ashamed; because the love of God is shed abroad in our hearts by the Holy Ghost which is given unto us. . . . For if, when we were enemies, we were reconciled to God by the death of his Son, much more, being reconciled, we shall be saved by his life" (Rom. 5:5,10).

"In whom ye also trusted, after that ye heard the word of truth, the gospel of your salvation: in whom also after that ye believed, ye were sealed with that holy Spirit of promise, which is the earnest of our inheritance until the redemption of the purchased possession, unto the praise of his glory" (Eph. 1:13,14; see also 3:16-20).

God has provided all that we need in order to live in victory over sin and thus please Him in all that we do. This is emphasized in II Peter 1:3,4: "According as his divine power hath given unto us all things that pertain unto life and godliness, through the knowledge of him that hath called us to glory and virtue: whereby are given unto us exceeding great and precious promises: that by these ye might be partakers of the divine nature, having escaped the corruption that is in the world through lust." In Hebrews 13:21 we learn that God works in us "that which is wellpleasing in his sight."

So we learn that Jesus Christ did something *for* us—He died on the cross to pay the penalty for our sin. But we also learn that Jesus Christ wants to do something *in* us, and it is important that we cooperate with Him in order to mature spiritually. God did something for Israel when He delivered them from Egypt, but in the desert He was working in them to accomplish His will in their lives.

When Jesus spoke with the woman at the well, He said, "Whosoever drinketh of the water that I shall give him shall never thirst; but the water that I shall give him shall be in him a well of water springing up into everlasting life" (John 4:14). Notice especially the words "in him." When we trust Jesus Christ as Saviour, He takes up residence in our lives to accomplish His will *in* us. Eternal life is like a well within us—it sustains our lives, for it is the life of Jesus Christ in us.

God Works Through the Believer

In the third stage of the believer's life with the Lord he is delivered from the disgrace of the self-life and is established as a mature, functioning vessel in the hands of the Holy Spirit. In this case, the Holy Spirit works *through* us. We choose to be the servants of the Lord, and thus we are His bondslaves, allowing Him to work through us. Jesus referred to His work in and through us when He said, "If any man thirst, let him come unto me, and drink. He that believeth on me, as the scripture hath said, out of his belly shall flow rivers of living water" (John 7:37,38). The Holy Spirit makes the things of Christ real to us and then works out the life of Christ through us. We must always remember that the Lord Jesus Christ cannot do His work *through* us until we allow Him to do His work *in* us.

The nation of Israel provides the sad example of how long it takes some to allow God to accomplish His purpose in their lives. The trip from Egypt to Canaan should have lasted no longer than two years at the most to provide all the training Israel needed. But because of disobedience the nation wandered 40 years in the wilderness before God could accomplish His purpose. As individual believers, we need to make sure that it doesn't take a long desert experience for us to learn the lessons God wants to teach us.

If we are to have victory over evil and the Evil One as we wrestle against principalities and powers, we need to obey the instructions of the Word of God. "Wherefore take unto you the whole armour of God, that ye may be able to withstand in the evil day, and having done all, to stand" (Eph. 6:13). The following verses list the armor that the believer is to put on—truth, the breastplate of righteousness, the preparation of the gospel of peace, the shield of faith, the helmet of salvation and the sword of the Spirit (vv. 14-17). All of this armor is necessary and is provided for the purpose of enabling us to be victorious in our spiritual warfare.

Consider also that the Lord Jesus Christ has ascended into heaven and has provided the Holy Spirit to live within each believer. It is important for us to get beyond just seeing what Christ has provided *for* us in delivering us from the guilt and condemnation of sin. This is tremendously significant and is foundational to all else, but we need to go beyond that stage in our lives with the Lord. God wanted far more for Israel than just to deliver them from Egypt; He wanted them to enter the land, to conquer it and to possess it by faith. Jesus Christ has given us the Holy Spirit to make us effective in all that we do for Him.

In Ephesians 1 the Apostle Paul prayed for believers, "That ye may know . . . what is the exceeding greatness of his power to us-ward who believe, according to the working of his mighty power" (vv. 18,19). This power is available to those who have trusted Jesus Christ as personal Saviour. Ephesians 2:5,6 reveals why we have such power—because of our position in Christ: "Even when we were dead in sins, hath quickened us together with Christ, (by grace ye are saved;) and hath raised us up together, and made us sit together in heavenly places in Christ Jesus."

Personal Emancipation

Have you really been emancipated from the guilt and condemnation of sin as the nation Israel was emancipated from Egypt? Have you trusted Jesus Christ as your personal Saviour? It does not matter how religious you are or how much religious activity you may be engaged in. The important question is, Have you personally placed your trust in Jesus Christ as your only hope for salvation? It's possible to be extremely religious and yet to be lost because no decision has been made to receive Christ as Saviour.

Do not make the mistake of thinking that a religious atmosphere or religious activities take the place of a personal relationship with Jesus Christ. In my own case, I was reared by wonderful Christian parents, so I had a religious atmosphere. But it wasn't until I was 20 years old that I really recognized that I was lost and needed to personally trust Jesus Christ as my Saviour. Outwardly, I did the things that are normally expected of Christians, but inwardly I had never made the decision to personally trust Christ. I was a member of a church, but I was not a member of the Body of Christ. In spite of all the religious atmosphere and activities, had I

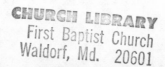

died in that condition, I would have spent eternity in hell because I had never personally believed on Christ for my salvation. I urge you to check your own heart to be sure of your relationship with the Lord.

Chapter 3

Saved by Blood

The process of God's redemption of Israel provides an example of how He redeems every sinner through the Lord Jesus Christ. Israel's redemption is beautifully divided into two aspects, helping us to clearly see all that is included in the great salvation God has provided for mankind.

Two Aspects of Redemption

The first aspect of God's redemption of Israel concerns blood. Exodus 12 records that each household was to kill a lamb and apply its blood to the upper and side posts of the door. Without the shedding and application of the blood every Israelite family would have lost the firstborn of their children and their animals. There was no deliverance without the shedding and application of the blood of a lamb.

This shedding of blood typifies the shedding of Christ's blood for the forgiveness of sin. Hebrews 9:22 says, "And almost all things are by the law purged with blood; and without shedding of blood is no remission [forgiveness]." The shed blood of Christ provides deliverance from condemnation for all who trust Him as Saviour. John 5:24 records the words of Christ regarding this matter: "He that heareth my word, and believeth on him that sent me, hath everlasting life, and shall not come into condemnation; but is passed from death unto life." Deliverance from condemnation is possible only because Christ shed His blood for us—"while we were yet sinners, Christ died for us" (Rom. 5:8).

19

What a significant parallel the individual believer's life is to the nation of Israel. The only means of deliverance from condemnation for the Israelites was the shedding and application of blood. Romans 8:1 proclaims, "There is therefore now no condemnation to them which are in Christ Jesus." First John 5:12 promises, "He that hath the Son hath life."

The second phase of salvation concerns power. By God's power He delivered the Israelites from the slavery of Egypt and then took them to the desert for training. There they had to depend totally on God's leadership and power for all of their needs.

So, too, the individual believer needs to rely totally on God for power in daily living. Salvation in Christ makes one a "new creature" (II Cor. 5:17), and the believer needs to realize that "all things are of God" (v. 18). God's leadership and power are provided for the believer in the death and resurrection of Jesus Christ and effected by the Holy Spirit who has been given to us.

The Scope of God's Judgment

God's sentence of judgment included the Israelites as well as the Egyptians: "All the firstborn in the land of Egypt shall die, from the firstborn of Pharaoh that sitteth upon his throne, even unto the firstborn of the maidservant that is behind the mill; and all the firstborn of beasts" (Ex. 11:5). This sentence of condemnation was designed particularly for the Egyptians, but even the Israelites could not escape the judgment unless a lamb was killed and its blood applied to the doorposts of their dwelling.

Israel could not escape this judgment simply because they were a righteous people or because they were a chosen people. They had to make personal application of the blood if they were to escape the sentence of judgment. The Israelites were direct descendants of Abraham, with whom God had made a covenant, but this special relationship alone did not exempt them from the judgment God was about to bring on all Egypt.

Many today think that because they have been reared in a godly home and have attended a good church they will escape condemnation. But these things in themselves do not deliver a person from condemnation. There must be a personal relationship with Jesus Christ—there must be a personal application of His blood in order for that individual to be delivered from condemnation. One born into a godly home is no different than one born into an ungodly home. This truth is evident from Romans 3:22,23: "For there is no difference: for all have sinned, and come short of the glory of God." This sentence of universal condemnation proceeds from the righteousness of God.

The words of Romans 3:23 cannot be emphasized too strongly: "All have sinned, and come short of the glory of God." Romans 6:23 states the results of serving sin: "For the wages of sin is death." However, verse 23 does not end with that statement. It goes on to say, "But the gift of God is eternal life through Jesus Christ our Lord."

Justice Satisfied; Mercy Expressed

God cannot clear the guilty unless the standards of His holiness are met. God wants to be merciful to us, but He cannot be merciful until His justice has been completely satisfied. The good news is that God's justice was completely satisfied in the death of His Son. Romans 3:24,25 tells us, "Being justified freely by his grace through the redemption that is in Christ Jesus: whom God hath set forth to be a propitiation through faith in his blood, to declare his righteousness for the remission of sins that are past, through the forbearance of God."

Because the Lord Jesus Christ satisfied the righteous demands of the Heavenly Father, it was possible for God to uphold His righteous standards and yet be able to forgive those who trusted Jesus Christ for salvation. This fact is expressed in Romans 3:26: "To declare, I say, at this time his righteousness: that he might be just, and the justifier of him which believeth in Jesus."

Justice and mercy were reconciled because justice was satisfied by the offering of the shed blood of Jesus. Every demand of justice was satisfied; every claim of holiness was fully met. All of this was possible by means of a substitute. Just as a lamb was offered as a sacrifice in Old Testament times, so Jesus Christ was the Lamb of God who took away the sin of the world (see John 1:29).

When God gave instructions to the Israelites prior to the Exodus from Egypt, He told Moses, "Speak ye unto all the congregation of Israel, saying, In the tenth day of this month they shall take to them every man a lamb, according to the house of their fathers, a lamb for an house: and if the household be too little for the lamb, let him and his neighbour next unto his house take it according to the number of the souls; every man according to his eating shall make your count for the lamb. Your lamb shall be without blemish, a male of the first year: ye shall take it out from the sheep, or from the goats" (Ex. 12:3-5). A lamb without blemish died and was accepted by God as a substitute for the firstborn.

The difference between the Egyptians and the Israelites was not a moral one because all were under sin. The difference was only the blood of the lamb. The Israelites experienced the mercy of God because they put their faith in the substitute, allowing God's justice to be satisfied so He could extend mercy. The meeting of justice and mercy was beautifully expressed by the psalmist: "Mercy and truth are met together; righteousness and peace have kissed each other" (Ps. 85:10). The meeting of justice and mercy is possible only because of shed blood. The Passover lamb was a type of Christ who shed His blood on the cross, thus becoming the Passover Lamb for the world.

Concerning Christ, the Lamb of God, the Bible says that the Father "hath made him to be sin for us, who knew no sin; that we might be made the righteousness of God in him" (II Cor. 5:21). Romans 8:32 adds, "He that spared not his own Son, but delivered him up for us all, how shall he not with him also freely give us all things?" All of this is available to us as believers because "we were reconciled to God by the death of his Son" (5:10).

No one is saved by prayer, although prayer is a way of accepting salvation or expressing our desire for it. Neither is anyone saved by fasting. Rather, salvation is only by substitution—trusting Jesus Christ as Saviour because He is the One who died in the place of every person. People are saved not because of any righteousness they have in themselves but because of trusting in Jesus Christ, who then becomes their righteousness.

Application of the Blood

So, also, the Israelites were not spared judgment in Egypt because they prayed or because they fasted or because of their own merits but only because they applied the shed blood as God instructed. They were in houses behind the blood which had been applied to the doorposts; thus, their firstborn were spared from death.

In order for the firstborn to be spared, a lamb had to be killed and its blood applied to the doorposts. Death would be inflicted either on the firstborn or on the substitute for the firstborn. But the death of the lamb alone would not do; its blood had to be applied as God instructed. God said, "They shall take of the blood, and strike it on the two side posts and on the upper door post of the houses" (Ex. 12:7). Nothing was left to chance or to man's ingenuity. Salvation was, and is, totally of God.

Hebrews 9:22 says, "Without shedding of blood is no remission [forgiveness]." But in Exodus 12:7 God instructed that the blood be sprinkled on the doorposts. Do these terms refer to the same action? No, shedding and sprinkling are not synonymous. The shedding of blood refers to propitiation, or satisfaction. Sprinkling of blood refers to appropriation, or application.

Although Christ shed His blood for the sins of the world (I John 2:2), no one is saved from condemnation unless he personally trusts Christ as Saviour (John 1:12). Receiving Christ as Saviour is appropriating to oneself what Christ has made available. Not until the blood has been applied does it actually provide safety. It is not enough to know that the blood of Jesus Christ was shed for the forgiveness of sin—one must personally trust Him as Saviour.

Just as none of the Israelites were delivered from death simply by the shedding of the lamb's blood, so no one is delivered from eternal condemnation just by the shedding of Christ's blood. In both cases the blood must be applied. There must be "faith in his blood" (Rom. 3:25). Forgiveness and reconciliation are attained by faith only—"For by grace

are ye saved through faith; and that not of yourselves: it is
the gift of God: not of works, lest any man should boast"
(Eph. 2:8,9).

Notice that the sprinkling of blood by the Israelites was
not to be a secretive thing—it was to be sprinkled on the
doorposts, indicating public, or open, confession. The New
Testament says that "if thou shalt confess with thy mouth
the Lord Jesus, and shalt believe in thine heart that God hath
raised him from the dead, thou shalt be saved" (Rom. 10:9).

The Israelites were not to sprinkle the blood on the
threshold where it might be trampled on but on the doorposts as a public confession. This was also God's seal for
them, which promised that they would be spared the judgment of death on the firstborn.

God made it unmistakably clear to the Israelites what it
would take for them to escape judgment: "When I see the
blood, I will pass over you, and the plague shall not be upon
you to destroy you, when I smite the land of Egypt" (Ex.
12:13). Unless the Israelites met God's conditions, they
would experience the loss of their firstborn just as the
Egyptians would. So it was necessary for each family to
apply the shed blood of a lamb to the doorposts. The applied
blood was the only means of safety. It revealed that deliverance had already been accomplished in the death of the
substitute. God's eye was not on the house as such nor on
those in it but on the blood which had been applied to the
house.

Feelings and God's Promises

Have you ever wondered how those in the house might
have felt during this time? Even after they had sprinkled the
blood on the doorposts, could they be sure that they would
escape God's judgment on the land of Egypt?

A similar question which many ask today is, How can a
person be sure of his relationship with God? Each person
should ask himself, What am I depending on for my salvation?

The only correct answer to both questions is, One can
depend on the promises of God. It did not matter how the
Israelites felt. Feelings had nothing to do with their deliver-

ance. The crucial matter was whether they had taken God at
His word and had applied the blood. If so, they could also
count on His promise to deliver them from the judgment
regardless of their feelings at the time.

So, too, when a person today applies the shed blood of
Christ by trusting Him as personal Saviour, he can count on
the promises of God to deliver him from coming judgment. A
person must not rely on his family or church background or
on anything else. Salvation is obtained only by applying the
shed blood of Christ, which is done by receiving Him as
personal Saviour. When this is done, one can then rely on
Christ's promise: "He that heareth my word, and believeth
on him that sent me, hath everlasting life, and shall not come
into condemnation; but is passed from death unto life" (John
5:24). Notice that the one who has trusted Christ as Saviour
will never come into condemnation. What a tremendous
promise!

The assurance of salvation is not based on some special
feeling; rather, it is to be based on God's promises. We are to
take God at His word. Satan tries to get a person to trust his
feelings, because he knows that the person will probably
doubt his salvation as soon as his feelings change. But if you
have trusted Jesus Christ as your personal Saviour, you are a
child of God—you have forgiveness of sin and eternal life
whether you feel like it or not!

When the lamb had been slain and the blood applied to
the doorposts, no one could condemn the Israelites. So, also,
because Christ had been crucified for the world, and when
His blood is applied by individually receiving Him as Saviour,
a person is delivered from condemnation (John 5:24). These
are promises that God Himself has made, and it is "impossible for God to lie" (Heb. 6:18).

When a person appropriates what God has done for him,
no one can successfully bring a charge against him. The Bible
says, "Who shall lay anything to the charge of God's elect? It
is God that justifieth. Who is he that condemneth? It is Christ
that died, yea rather, that is risen again, who is even at the
right hand of God, who also maketh intercession for us"
(Rom. 8:33,34). Christ has accomplished all that we need for
salvation, and He is at the right hand of God this very

moment interceding for those who have trusted Him as Saviour.

Concerning the importance of the sacrifice of the Lord Jesus Christ, Hebrews 10:14 says, "For by one offering he hath perfected for ever them that are sanctified." The Old Testament offerings had to be made over and over again, but the offering of Christ for sin was made once for all.

Since Christ was the offering for sin, anyone who places his faith in Jesus Christ as his Saviour is delivered from condemnation. However, even though we are saved by faith (Eph. 2:8,9), we are not to think that faith *itself* saves. It is actually the object of our faith—the Lord Jesus Christ—that saves us. Faith itself has not paid the penalty for sin. Only Jesus Christ has paid this penalty; faith is the means by which we appropriate what He accomplished.

If no blood was on the doorposts of the houses of the Israelites, no amount of believing that it was there would deliver the occupants from judgment. They actually had to put their confidence in God's word and then act accordingly. Just believing that Jesus Christ lived long ago and died for our sin does not save anyone from condemnation; an individual must personally trust Jesus Christ as his Saviour in order to be saved. Once this decision for Christ has been made, a person is saved regardless of his feelings or uncertainties, just as the Israelites were delivered from judgment by applying the blood regardless of how many questions they may have had.

It is important to distinguish between security and assurance. A person who trusts Christ as Saviour has security whether he realizes it or not (John 10:28,29). Assurance is that peace of heart that comes from taking God at His word concerning one's security. Assurance is related to peace about one's relationship with the Lord.

Satan loves to destroy a person's peace concerning his security in Christ. But the Christian who has confidence in God's Word will have assurance about his salvation because he is resting on the promises of God, not on feelings. Although peace may be destroyed, security depends on the promises of God. Assurance is the response of a person's heart, acknowledging by faith that what God has said is true.

Instructions to the Israelites

Consider the various aspects of the instructions God gave the Israelites prior to the Exodus. The blood made them safe; the word made them sure. The feast which they were instructed to eat made them strong; the dress (they were instructed to eat fully clothed) made them ready for departure. These truths are seen in Exodus 12:8-11.

All of this has a modern-day parallel. It is not enough that Christ has died on the cross—we must appropriate by faith what He has done for us. By faith He becomes our life, and by faith we receive strength from Him. Such was alluded to by Jesus Himself, as recorded in John 6:51,54: "I am the living bread which came down from heaven: if any man eat of this bread, he shall live for ever: and the bread that I will give is my flesh, which I will give for the life of the world. . . . Whoso eateth my flesh, and drinketh my blood, hath eternal life; and I will raise him up at the last day."

Concerning the eating of the lamb, God instructed the Israelites, "Thus shall ye eat it; with your loins girded, your shoes on your feet, and your staff in your hand; and ye shall eat it in haste: it is the Lord's passover" (Ex. 12:11). The lamb was to be eaten for strength and in a posture that was ready for departure. The Israelites were to shake off the yoke of Egypt and forsake the sin of the land. They were citizens of another country and were to be ready to leave immediately for that land.

This reminds us of Hebrews 13:12-14: "Wherefore Jesus also, that he might sanctify the people with his own blood, suffered without the gate. Let us go forth therefore unto him without the camp, bearing his reproach. For here have we no continuing city, but we seek one to come."

Second Corinthians 6:14 also instructs believers, "Be ye not unequally yoked together with unbelievers: for what fellowship hath righteousness with unrighteousness? And what communion hath light with darkness?" So even though the believer is *in* the world he is not to be part *of* the world—he is to be separated to God even while living in the world.

From Exodus 12:34-37 we learn more details about the activities of Israel: "So the people took their dough before it was leavened, with their kneading bowls bound up in the clothes on their shoulders. Now the sons of Israel had done according to the word of Moses, for they had requested from the Egyptians articles of silver and articles of gold, and clothing; and the Lord had given the people favor in the sight of the Egyptians, so that they let them have their request. Thus they plundered the Egyptians. Now the sons of Israel journeyed from Rameses to Succoth, about six hundred thousand men on foot, aside from children" (NASB).

Just as the Israelites were to move out at once from Egypt, so the person who knows Jesus Christ as Saviour should immediately begin a journey away from the things of the world. This present world should not be considered home by believers. The Bible says, "For here have we no continuing city, but we seek one to come" (Heb. 13:14).

Abraham was an example to the believer in the way he should fix his eyes on eternal, not temporal, blessings. The Bible says concerning Abraham, "By faith he sojourned in the land of promise, as in a strange country, dwelling in tabernacles with Isaac and Jacob, the heirs with him of the same promise: for he looked for a city which hath foundations, whose builder and maker is God" (11:9,10). Philippians 3:20 tells believers, "For our conversation [citizenship] is in heaven; from whence also we look for the Saviour, the Lord Jesus Christ."

God does not expect the believer to leave this world, but He expects him to be separated from it while he is here. In His high-priestly prayer the Lord Jesus said, "I pray not that thou shouldest take them out of the world, but that thou shouldest keep them from the evil [one]" (John 17:15).

So we see that the first step of God's redemption was to save them by blood. However, the Israelites also needed to be delivered from slavery to the Egyptians. This was the second step in God's redemptive plan for them.

Chapter 4

Saved by Power

As the Israelites began their march, God began to deal with them in the second phase of His redemptive plan, a step that involved power. Although these were distinct steps in Israel's deliverance, the steps involving blood and power take place simultaneously today when an individual becomes a Christian. When one receives Jesus Christ as his Saviour, the blood of Christ is applied to his life—the benefit of what Christ accomplished is applied to him. At the same time, God gives the believer power to live a life separated from the world.

Having clearly instructed the Israelites to apply the blood to the doorposts, God began to lead them through the wilderness. Exodus 12:37 says, "And the children of Israel journeyed from Rameses to Succoth, about six hundred thousand on foot that were men, beside children." Inasmuch as wives and children were not counted in these 600,000, it is estimated that the total group may have been between two and three million people.

They journeyed "from Rameses to Succoth." This was a journey of about 15 miles and was on a well-traveled trade route that would lead them directly to Canaan. It was about 200 miles from where they had lived in Egypt to the land of Canaan, and this trade route could be traveled in about eight or ten days. Traders who traveled the road could make the distance in about three days, but a huge group like the Israelites would take much longer.

This part of the journey was initiated by the people themselves under the leadership of Moses. Succoth made a good meeting place for them before proceeding further to Canaan.

The Bible says, "They baked unleavened cakes of the dough which they brought forth out of Egypt, for it was not leavened; because they were thrust out of Egypt, and could not tarry, neither had they prepared for themselves any victual" (v. 39). This verse reveals how quickly the Israelites left Egypt.

Note the statement, "And a mixed multitude went up also with them" (v. 38). This mixed multitude that went along with the Israelites later proved to be one of the wiles of the Devil, who operates both as a roaring lion and as a cunning serpent. In Egypt he had worked as a roaring lion through the oppression of Pharaoh and his attempts to keep the Israelites in Egypt. But when Satan was unable to keep the Israelites in Egypt, he tried to hinder their clean separation from Egypt by an infiltration of those who were not really believers.

Later on, there were possibly intermarriages of this mixed multitude with the Israelites. Those who were not really believers proved to be a thorn in Israel's side because they became dissatisfied and influenced the Israelites to grumble time and again. This mixed multitude reminds us of the unconverted who attend church services today. If they are allowed a voice of authority in the church, they most certainly will direct the church in a way that is not honoring to God.

The mixed multitude apparently had been drawn to the Israelites because of the demonstration of divine power, yet they had not really experienced a change of heart. They saw that something was happening to the Israelites, and they wanted to be a part of it even though they did not have a proper relationship with the Lord.

God's Route

The Israelites traveled from Rameses to Succoth, but then God chose a different route for them. The Bible says, "And it came to pass, when Pharaoh had let the people go, that God led them not through the way of the land of the Philistines, although that was near; for God said, Lest peradventure the people repent when they see war, and they return to Egypt: but God led the people about, through the way of the wilderness of the Red sea: and the children of Israel went up harnessed out of the land of Egypt" (Ex. 13:17,18). The route God chose was not by an easily traveled road but was a detour through the wilderness. The other road led through a populated area; it was easier and much more traveled, but in His wisdom, God chose the long road for the Israelites.

On this long route there were no highways, no bridges, no resources to supply their needs and no signs to direct their paths. In fact, it took them two years to reach Kadesh-barnea, which was on the southern extremity of the land of Canaan. But even this teaches us that God chooses the way His people should go. There is a very important lesson to be learned from this incident. We should not only realize that God chooses the way, but we should recognize that it is for our best if we respond to His direction.

Jeremiah said, "O Lord, I know that the way of man is not in himself: it is not in man that walketh to direct his steps" (Jer. 10:23). Proverbs 20:24 says, "Man's goings are of the Lord; how can a man then understand his own way?"

Realizing that we do not have the wisdom to know for sure the way we should walk, it is important that we rely on the counsel of God's Word. "Trust in the Lord with all thine heart; and lean not unto thine own understanding. In all thy ways acknowledge him, and he shall direct thy paths. Be not wise in thine own eyes: fear the Lord, and depart from evil" (3:5-7).

Notice also Psalm 37:23: "The steps of a good man are ordered by the Lord: and he delighteth in his way." Psalm 119:105 says, "Thy word is a lamp unto my feet, and a light unto my path." The New Testament assures, "For as many as are led by the Spirit of God, they are the sons of God" (Rom. 8:14).

By blood the Israelites had been delivered from the judgment on the firstborn. By the power of God they had been delivered from slavery in Egypt. Now they were being led by God, not on the easily traveled, short route, but on the difficult, long road.

Chapter 5

The Long Road

"It came to pass, when Pharaoh had let the people go, that God led them not through the way of the land of the Philistines, although that was near; for God said, Lest peradventure the people repent when they see war, and they return to Egypt: but God led the people about, through the way of the wilderness of the Red sea: and the children of Israel went up harnessed out of the land of Egypt" (Ex. 13:17,18).

Preparation for Warfare

In a sense, the Israelites were God's infant children, and from the standpoints of traveling and warfare they had many things to learn. And through the experiences of the nation of Israel, God has many things to teach those of us who live today. The New Testament says, "Now all these things happened unto them for ensamples [examples]: and they are written for our admonition, upon whom the ends of the world are come" (I Cor. 10:11).

This same passage tells us, "There hath no temptation taken you but such as is common to man: but God is faithful, who will not suffer [permit] you to be tempted above that ye are able; but will with the temptation also make a way to escape, that ye may be able to bear it" (v. 13). This verse is not only true concerning us, but it was also true concerning the Israelites. God was not going to submit them to a test more difficult than they could bear. God knows how much we can take; therefore, He knows how many tests to allow to come into our lives in order to help us to mature.

God completely understands us, so He knows our feelings when we face difficult situations. Psalm 103 expresses this so well, and over the years I've gone back to this psalm hundreds of times. Especially notice verses 13 and 14: "Like as a father pitieth his children, so the Lord pitieth them that fear him. For he knoweth our frame; he remembereth that we are dust."

Abraham is a prime example of biblical characters who passed through tests. God allowed him to pass through many tests of faith until He brought him to the last and greatest test—the offering of his son. The rest of the tests were mild in comparison to that, but they grew more severe as God sought to mature Abraham in the faith.

Although God may never ask us to literally sacrifice a son, He does bring greater and greater tests into our lives in order to mature us and to conform us "to the image of his Son" (Rom. 8:29).

Israel was not yet ready for warfare, yet later they would be fighting the Canaanites. So it was necessary for God to allow the nation to be tested in order to prepare them for battle.

The Christian is involved in spiritual warfare, and God has supplied all of his needs for that. Ephesians 1:3 tells of God's supply: "Blessed be the God and Father of our Lord Jesus Christ, who hath blessed us with all spiritual blessings in heavenly places in Christ." But God is concerned that we apply what He has made available for us. This passage goes on to say, "According as he hath chosen us in him before the foundation of the world, that we should be holy and without blame before him in love: having predestinated us unto the adoption of children by Jesus Christ to himself, according to the good pleasure of his will, to the praise of the glory of his grace, wherein he hath made us accepted in the beloved" (vv. 4-6).

The Book of Ephesians climaxes by telling of the warfare in which the maturing Christian will be engaged: "Finally, my brethren, be strong in the Lord, and in the power of his might. Put on the whole armour of God, that ye may be able to stand against the wiles of the devil. For we wrestle not against flesh and blood, but against principalities, against powers, against the rulers of the darkness of this world, against spiritual wickedness in high places" (6:10-12).

In spiritual warfare it is very important for us to learn that God never asks us to bear more than we are able, just as He never called on the Israelites to bear more than they were able.

God intended the long road by which He led the Israelites to be a means of blessing them rather than a means of withholding blessing. We often assume that the shortcut always holds the blessing rather than the long road, but this only reveals that we look at things from the human standpoint rather than from God's viewpoint. Sometimes detours are more beautiful than the main road. But even if no physical beauty is involved, there is beauty of soul when God accomplishes His purpose in an individual life.

It is important to remember that God led the Israelites— He selected the way. Nothing was left to chance or to poor reasoning. God had brought Israel into existence by His own choice; now He was leading the people in the way they should go.

Concerning Christians today, the New Testament reveals: "We are his workmanship, created in Christ Jesus unto good works, which God hath before ordained that we should walk in them" (Eph. 2:10). We are created for good works, and God works in our lives in order to lead us on to spiritual maturity (1:4,5).

The blessing in God's leading Israel Himself can be seen as one considers that these people had been slaves in Egypt. They were undisciplined in the art of warfare and survival—all they knew was the hard work of slavery.

God wanted the nation of Israel to have a walk of faith, not a walk based only on sight. The only way He could teach them this was by means of the long road. They had to learn to wait on God; they had to learn to be patient; they had to learn to trust God completely.

Although we cannot always understand God's providential workings, we can learn to believe and trust Him. This comes from realizing that God, in His wisdom, makes no mistakes and that the final outcome will be for our good and His glory.

Five Purposes of the Long Road

There were at least five purposes of the long road for Israel. First, it was used to reveal God's power as He led them through the Red Sea, not around it. The people had to experience the great power of God in doing spectacular things for them. By opening the Red Sea for them, God revealed His tremendous power so that they could trust Him for anything in the future.

Second, the long route was used to destroy the power of the enemy. When the Israelites had passed through the Red Sea, the water closed in on the Egyptians, their enemy. At that time Israel recognized the wonderful power of God.

Third, while on the long road Israel received the Law. In God's program of the ages there was a specific time and a specific place for the Mosaic Law to be given. The Israelites were the specific people to receive it, and God wanted them in the place of His choice for this purpose.

Fourth, the Israelites had time to become properly organized. The children of Israel needed to be organized into a commonwealth prior to their entrance into Canaan.

Fifth, Israel was humbled and proved on the long road. The desert was the only place large enough that would provide a place where the Israelites could be completely separated to God.

Later, in speaking to the children who had come through the wilderness experience, Moses told them, "Thou shalt remember all the way which the Lord thy God led thee these forty years in the wilderness, to humble thee, and to prove thee, to know what was in thine heart, whether thou wouldest keep his commandments, or no. And he humbled thee, and suffered thee to hunger, and fed thee with manna, which thou knewest not, neither did thy fathers know; that he might make thee know that man doth not live by bread only, but by every word that proceedeth out of the mouth of the Lord doth man live" (Deut. 8:2,3).

Israel needed to learn God's way of working with His people. They needed to learn what was later stated in Romans 8:28: "We know that all things work together for good to them that love God, to them who are the called according to his purpose." The reason for God's working this way is seen in the following verse: "For whom he did foreknow, he also did predestinate to be conformed to the image of his Son" (v. 29). God wants believers to be conformed to the image of Jesus Christ.

Even though the Israelites did not have the New Testament, they had sufficient information about God to realize that He knew best and that only when they followed Him would things work out to their good and for His glory.

The Israelites also needed to learn something about the way God deals with His own in chastisement. This is a method God uses to train His children and mature them. Concerning chastening Hebrews 12:5-7 says, "Despise not thou the chastening of the Lord, nor faint when thou art rebuked of him: for whom the Lord loveth he chasteneth, and scourgeth every son whom he receiveth. If ye endure chastening, God dealeth with you as with sons; for what son is he whom the father chasteneth not?" So when God chastens an individual, it reveals that the person really belongs to Him. This is God's way of dealing with His own children in order to train them and lead them on to spiritual maturity.

There is no indication that the chastening of the Lord is enjoyable; in fact, the opposite is true. Hebrews 12:11 says, "Now no chastening for the present seemeth to be joyous, but grievous: nevertheless afterward it yieldeth the peaceable fruit of righteousness unto them which are exercised thereby." This is what Israel had to learn, and this is what we have to learn also.

Knowing Themselves and Knowing God

The Israelites definitely needed to understand two other matters—they needed to know themselves and they needed to know God.

God led them 40 years in the wilderness for the purpose of helping them to know themselves. There He humbled them and proved them so they would know what was in their hearts (Deut. 8:2).

After the Apostle Paul learned what was in his heart, he wrote: "For I know that in me (that is, in my flesh,) dwelleth no good thing: for to will is present with me; but how to perform that which is good I find not" (Rom. 7:18). Paul had no confidence in the flesh. Most of us have to learn this lesson the hard way; Israel learned it in the wilderness.

The purpose of the Law that was later given to Israel was to reveal their sinfulness in order to emphasize how far they were from the standards of God. The ceremonial law revealed God's grace, however, for it made provision for sin.

God's leading and the instructions He gave the Israelites were to enable them to know themselves better. Out in the desert they were completely alone with God and were forced to see themselves as they really were. They had to learn to depend on Him to supply their needs.

In addition to learning to know themselves, the Israelites also needed to learn to know God. They needed to personally experience how God can take care of His own. Moses reminded the Israelites of the way God worked with them when he said, "He humbled thee, and suffered thee to hunger, and fed thee with manna, which thou knewest not, neither did thy fathers know; that he might make thee know that man doth not live by bread only, but by every word that proceedeth out of the mouth of the Lord doth man live" (Deut. 8:3).

In order for the Israelites to really know God, they had to follow Him. They had seen how God had miraculously worked at the Passover, but they had many other things to experience in the wilderness that would prove God's ability to take care of His own. In the wilderness they were to see how God would provide food and water, protect them from the enemy and reveal His Law to them. All these things were necessary for them to really learn to know God.

These were not things that Israel could learn on the easy road; the path of least resistance never teaches the valuable lessons that one needs to know. Too many Christians are unwilling to let God deal with their souls because they do not realize the good that can result. Perhaps they even want to know God better, but they are unwilling to be really exercised about spiritual matters.

The Long Road Brings Blessing

In the wilderness God revealed Himself to the Israelites so they would have a firsthand knowledge of Him. Even though the longer way may have seemed harder to the Israelites, it was really the way of comfort and advantage. Notice the significant words in Exodus 13:18: "God led the people about." God led them through the trackless wilderness to make them totally dependent on Himself.

This is an important lesson for us to learn. God often leads His children through the deep, dark valleys to teach them His ways and to enable them to fully experience His blessing. The Apostle Paul realized this, and he stated his heart's desire in these words: "That I may know him, and the power of his resurrection, and the fellowship of his sufferings, being made conformable unto his death" (Phil. 3:10). What a tremendous statement! If we desire power like this, we must ask ourselves if we also desire the fellowship of His suffering that goes along with it.

David realized the way the Lord works in a believer's life and expressed it in these words: "Yea, though I walk through the valley of the shadow of death, I will fear no evil: for thou art with me; thy rod and thy staff they comfort me" (Ps. 23:4). Although some think that David wrote this psalm when he was a young shepherd, he seems to be looking back over his life and reflecting on how many times God had led him through the valley of the shadow of death. He had faced death on many occasions, but God had delivered him. Before he became king, Saul tried to put David to death, but God preserved David's life. Seeing God work in his behalf caused David to have a different perspective on living the rest of his days.

So the wilderness and the valley experiences prepare us for the road ahead. The Bible says that the Israelites "took their journey from Succoth, and encamped in Etham, in the edge of the wilderness" (Ex. 13:20). At this point they were still journeying on a well-traveled road, but from here the caravan road turned to the northeast and went along the Mediterranean Sea. The desert was south of them, and Etham was right at the edge of the desert. It was here that God definitely took over and ordered that they travel south instead of following the well-known road.

The Lord told Moses, "Speak unto the children of Israel, that they turn and encamp before Pi-hahiroth, between Migdol and the sea, over against Baal-zephon: before it shall ye encamp by the sea. For Pharaoh will say of the children of Israel, They are entangled in the land, the wilderness hath shut them in" (14:2,3).

All the green vegetation faded away into waste and sand as the Israelites turned southward. That's exactly what God wanted because He knew what Pharaoh would think—that the Israelites were hopelessly entangled in the wilderness and that he could easily overtake them. But God had a plan in mind that was far beyond anything that Pharaoh could even imagine!

Chapter 6

Led by a Cloud

The method God used to lead the Israelites is indicated in Exodus 13:21,22: "The Lord went before them by day in a pillar of a cloud, to lead them the way; and by night in a pillar of fire, to give them light; to go by day and night: he took not away the pillar of the cloud by day, nor the pillar of fire by night, from before the people."

The Pillar of Cloud and Fire

We are not told how this pillar was shaped—perhaps it looked like a huge umbrella with a point, extending down to the people. Whatever shape it had, it served God's purpose in guiding the people both day and night. It protected them from the hot sun during the day, and it gave light to them at night. What a wonderful provision God made for His own!

As sinners the Israelites needed a savior; as captives they needed a deliverer; but as pilgrims they needed a guide. The predominant function of the pillar of cloud was to guide the Israelites through the barren desert as they journeyed from Egypt to Canaan.

God has also provided a guide for believers today, although it is not a pillar of cloud. The guide God has provided is the Holy Spirit. Before Jesus left His disciples, He told them, "I will pray the Father, and he shall give you another Comforter, that he may abide with you for ever; even the Spirit of truth; whom the world cannot receive, because it seeth him not, neither knoweth him: but ye know him; for he dwelleth with you, and shall be in you" (John 14:16,17). Jesus also told His disciples concerning the Holy

40

Spirit, "When he, the Spirit of truth, is come, he will guide you into all truth: for he shall not speak of himself; but whatsoever he shall hear, that shall he speak: and he will shew you things to come" (16:13).

For the Israelites the pillar of cloud was a visible sign of the Lord's presence with them. Regardless of the circumstances during their journey, the cloud—the evidence of God's presence—remained with them. How reassuring this must have been!

Fire is a symbol of the presence of the Lord, the One who neither sleeps nor slumbers. God gave abundant evidence of His presence—the pillar of cloud by day and the pillar of fire by night. At no time were the Israelites left without an evidence of His presence.

God's special care of Israel in the wilderness is indicated by what Moses said after the wilderness wanderings: "For the Lord's portion is his people; Jacob is the lot of his inheritance. He found him in a desert land, and in the waste howling wilderness; he led him about, he instructed him, he kept him as the apple of his eye. As an eagle stirreth up her nest, fluttereth over her young, spreadeth abroad her wings, taketh them, beareth them on her wings: so the Lord alone did lead him, and there was no strange god with him" (Deut. 32:9-12).

The appearance of the cloud to the Israelites in the desert marked a turning point in their journey. Exodus 13:20 says, "They took their journey from Succoth." The emphasis in this clause seems to be on what the Israelites did on their own. However, the following verse says, "The Lord went before them by day in a pillar of a cloud, to lead them the way" (v. 21). This indicates the intervention of the Lord in specifically leading the people in the way He wanted them to go.

When God began to lead them by a pillar of cloud by day and a pillar of fire by night, Israel's walk of faith really began. They were to move when the cloud moved, and they were to stay when the cloud remained stationary. They were to depend totally on the Lord for leadership.

Just as the cloud went before the Israelites, the Lord goes before those who are His own. The Bible says, "When he putteth forth his own sheep, he goeth before them, and the sheep follow him: for they know his voice" (John 10:4).

Inasmuch as God provided a pillar of fire at night for the Israelites, anyone who was not walking in the light evidenced that he was outside the realm of fellowship with the Israelites and with God. A parallel to this is seen in the New Testament: "God is light, and in him is no darkness at all. If we say that we have fellowship with him, and walk in darkness, we lie, and do not the truth: but if we walk in the light, as he is in the light, we have fellowship one with another, and the blood of Jesus Christ his Son cleanseth us from all sin" (I John 1:5-7).

Other writers in the Bible knew of the way God led the Israelites and wrote of it. Nehemiah wrote: "Moreover thou leddest them in the day by a cloudy pillar; and in the night by a pillar of fire, to give them light in the way wherein they should go" (Neh. 9:12). As we have indicated, God's guiding the Israelites by light is a reminder to us of His giving the Holy Spirit to guide believers "into all truth" (John 16:13).

The fact that God provided guidance for Israel revealed that they were His own people. He does not provide guidance for those who are not His own. So, also, Church-Age believers are told, "For as many as are led by the Spirit of God, they are the sons of God" (Rom. 8:14).

The Trumpets

In God's program of providing guidance for Israel, He later designated that trumpets be used for certain signals. God instructed, "Make thee two trumpets of silver; of a whole piece shalt thou make them: that thou mayest use them for the calling of the assembly, and for the journeying of the camps. And when they shall blow with them, all the assembly shall assemble themselves to thee at the door of the tabernacle of the congregation" (Num. 10:2,3). So in addition to the moving of the cloud, the Israelites had trumpets to signal them in their march through the wilderness.

Whereas the cloud reminds us of the leadership of the Holy Spirit, the trumpets remind us of the guidance of God's Word. The psalmist said, "Thy word is a lamp unto my feet, and a light unto my path" (Ps. 119:105). He also wrote:

"The entrance of thy words giveth light; it giveth understanding unto the simple" (v. 130). So the Word of God is to
be used as a guide—God never leads in a way that is contrary
to His revealed Word.

Trumpets are mentioned frequently in scripture—Israel
was guided by trumpets, and one trumpet in particular is
mentioned for the Church. Referring to the latter, the Bible
says, "For the Lord himself shall descend from heaven with a
shout, with the voice of the archangel, and with the trump
[trumpet] of God: and the dead in Christ shall rise first: then
we which are alive and remain shall be caught up together
with them in the clouds, to meet the Lord in the air: and so
shall we ever be with the Lord" (I Thess. 4:16,17).

Referring to the same event, I Corinthians 15:51,52 says,
"Behold, I shew you a mystery; We shall not all sleep, but we
shall all be changed, in a moment, in the twinkling of an eye,
at the last trump [trumpet] : for the trumpet shall sound, and
the dead shall be raised incorruptible, and we shall be
changed."

For Israel the cloud and the trumpets went together.
They were not led just by the cloud nor just by the trumpets
but by both. Of course, both would be in harmony if the
trumpets were blown according to God's direction.

Guidance of the Holy Spirit and God's Word

Some today want to be guided only by the cloud—the
leadership of the Holy Spirit. But it is evident that the
impressions they have do not always originate with the Holy
Spirit. Others want to be guided only by the trumpets—the
Word of God. They open the Bible at random and find a
verse on which they base a major decision. We must remember, however, that the cloud and the trumpets go together—
there must be the leading of both the Holy Spirit and the
Word of God. It is important to realize, however, that the
Holy Spirit never leads in a way that is contrary to what God
has revealed in His Word. As we study the Word, the Holy
Spirit will communicate to us what we ought to do.

The cloud God provided for Israel served as a covering for
the people. The psalmist said of God, "He spread a cloud for
a covering" (Ps. 105:39). From Exodus 14:19,20 we also

learn that the cloud served as a guard: "The angel of God, which went before the camp of Israel, removed and went behind them; and the pillar of the cloud went from before their face, and stood behind them: and it came between the camp of the Egyptians and the camp of Israel; and it was a cloud of darkness to them, but it gave light by night to these: so that the one came not near the other all the night."

On the one hand the cloud was a visible evidence of God's presence, but on the other hand it protected Israel from its enemies. The time referred to in this passage is when the Egyptians were pursuing the Israelites immediately after Moses had led them out of the land. But the conflict here was not so much between Israel and Egypt as it was between Jehovah and Egypt.

All the Israelites had to do was to remain in their place while God protected them. God put Himself between His own people and the enemy. God provided security for His own, even as we read in Ephesians 4:30 that we are sealed by the Holy Spirit for the day of redemption.

It is assuring to know that the child of God is under the protecting hand of God. This does not mean that the believer will be free from difficulty, however. "In the world," Jesus said, "ye shall have tribulation: but be of good cheer; I have overcome the world" (John 16:33). Jesus also promised, "I will never leave thee, nor forsake thee" (Heb. 13:5). Because of this great promise, believers can "boldly say, The Lord is my helper, and I will not fear what man shall do unto me" (v. 6).

The Israelites experienced the gracious provision of God—He never took away the pillar of cloud by day nor the pillar of fire by night (Ex. 13:22). In spite of all of the grumbling of Israel, God did not take away the visible signs of His presence. Concerning these experiences Nehemiah wrote: "Yet thou in thy manifold mercies forsookest them not in the wilderness: the pillar of the cloud departed not from them by day, to lead them in the way; neither the pillar of fire by night, to shew them light, and the way wherein they should go" (Neh. 9:19). Although God had to chasten the Israelites and even judge them at times, He never forsook them.

In Old Testament times it was possible for God to remove the Holy Spirit from people. This is why, after his sin, David prayed, "Take not thy holy spirit from me" (Ps. 51:11). This did not mean that the Old Testament believer lost his salvation. It meant only that God was removing the Holy Spirit from him for empowering him for a particular service. However, during the Church Age the Holy Spirit is never taken from the believer. Jesus promised that He would send the Holy Spirit "that he may abide with you for ever" (John 14:16).

The cloud that God provided for Israel's guidance is mentioned nearly 50 times in the Pentateuch alone and is frequently mentioned throughout other portions of the Bible. So the provision of the cloud was considered by Old Testament writers to be a highly significant matter in Israel's history. How wonderful it is to recognize that God leads His own people! He does not leave them to flounder on their own.

Chapter 7

Passing Through the Sea

Israel had congregated at a place called Succoth, which was located on a well-traveled route to Canaan. They were on their way to Etham, but somewhere between Succoth and Etham God took over the leadership and provided a cloud that stayed with them during the rest of their journey. But God's route took them a different direction than they had intended to go. They must have intended to go northeast on the well-traveled route, but God took them southeast into the wilderness. But as we have seen, God had reasons for taking them in this direction, for it was for their good and His glory.

What a beautiful sight it must have been as Israel traveled under the pillar of cloud by day and the pillar of fire by night! In the wilderness the Israelites had to depend completely on God's guidance and provision. They were able to see Him work in a way they otherwise never would have.

In all of this we see how God's preparation of His servant Moses paid off. How could any man lead so many people to and through the desert had not his faith in God been thoroughly settled? Moses showed that he had no doubts concerning God's ability to do what He purposed to do.

Hemmed in by Trials

Even as God had the Israelites turn south into the wilderness, He knew what Pharaoh would think: "For Pharaoh will say of the children of Israel, They are entangled in the land, the wilderness hath shut them in. And I will harden Pharaoh's heart, that he shall follow after them; and I will be honoured upon Pharaoh, and upon all his host; that the Egyptians may know that I am the Lord" (Ex. 14:3,4). Although Satan is wise, he is not as wise as God is, and time and time again Satan oversteps himself. This is what happened in Pharaoh's case. Pharaoh thought he could easily overtake the Israelites, so he and his army immediately pursued them (vv. 5-9). As the Egyptians came in behind them, the Israelites were terribly frightened, but they were about to see a great display of God's power.

We must remember that the Israelites were hemmed in on all sides. In front of them was the Red Sea, on the sides were mountains and the desert, and behind them were the pursuing Egyptians.

Have you had those times in your life when it seemed as if you had no place to turn except to God? Notice what the Bible says about trials that believers experience. First Peter 1:5-7 says that believers "are kept by the power of God through faith unto salvation ready to be revealed in the last time. Wherein ye greatly rejoice, though now for a season, if need be, ye are in heaviness through manifold temptations: that the trial of your faith, being much more precious than of gold that perisheth, though it be tried with fire, might be found unto praise and honour and glory at the appearing of Jesus Christ." Notice especially the words "the trial of your faith." To God it is very important that our faith be tested in order to prove its genuineness. We are not tested to see whether or not we have faith, but to reveal to us that the faith we have in Christ Jesus is the answer to our need.

The New Testament Epistle of James also tells about trials which believers undergo: "My brethren, count it all joy when ye fall into divers [various] temptations; knowing this, that the trying of your faith worketh patience. But let patience have her perfect work, that ye may be perfect and entire, wanting nothing. If any of you lack wisdom, let him ask of God, that giveth to all men liberally, and upbraideth not; and it shall be given him. But let him ask in faith, nothing wavering. For he that wavereth is like the wave of the sea driven with the wind and tossed" (1:2-6). If you wonder about the reason for your trials, turn to God and He will give you wisdom concerning what He is endeavoring to accomplish in your life.

God's reason for leading Israel by way of the long road was that He knew they would become discouraged if they got into war with the Philistines, and they would probably want to return to Egypt. Actually, the Israelites seemed to complain and wanted to return to Egypt every time things got difficult, but God knew it would have been worse had they gone the other way. How regrettable that the Israelites did not have enough confidence in God to realize that He would not test them beyond what they were able to bear (see I Cor. 10:13).

As we consider all that God allowed Israel to experience, it is understandable to ask the question, Why? The answer is given in I Corinthians 10:11: "All these things happened unto them for ensamples [examples]: and they are written for our admonition, upon whom the ends of the world are come." The experiences of Israel are typical of an individual Christian's experience, so the more a believer learns about the life of the nation of Israel, the more he will know about handling the difficulties that come into his own life.

Identification With God's Power

God made a unique display of His power when He opened the Red Sea and allowed the Israelites to pass through. So great was this demonstration of power that when Old Testament writers wanted to refer to God's tremendous power, they would cite the incident of the Red Sea. In the New Testament God's tremendous power was displayed in the resurrection of Jesus Christ, and the New Testament writers frequently referred to this incident when citing God's power.

The opening of the Red Sea and the resurrection of Christ are events which are appealed to as standards of measurement for the great power of God. Referring to the resurrection, Ephesians 1:19,20 says, "And what is the exceeding greatness of his power to us-ward who believe, according to the working of his mighty power, which he wrought in Christ, when he raised him from the dead." God raised Jesus from the dead in spite of the resistance of Satan and all the powers of hell who tried to keep Christ in the grave.

The New Testament also refers back to the Red Sea incident as a display of God's power. The Apostle Paul wrote: "Moreover, brethren, I would not that ye should be ignorant, how that all our fathers were under the cloud, and all passed through the sea; and were all baptized unto Moses in the cloud and in the sea" (I Cor. 10:1,2). The basic meaning of the word "baptized" here is "identified." The Israelites were delivered because they were identified with Moses in the Red Sea.

Baptism for the believer is an outward act which reveals his identification with Jesus Christ. Upon receiving Jesus Christ as Saviour, the Holy Spirit places the person into the Body of Christ. This is known as the baptism of the Holy Spirit (I Cor. 12:13).

Teaching concerning our identification with Christ through baptism is seen in Romans 6:4,5: "Therefore we are buried with him by baptism into death: that like as Christ was raised up from the dead by the glory of the Father, even so we also should walk in newness of life. For if we have been planted together in the likeness of his death, we shall be also in the likeness of his resurrection." Water baptism is simply a picture of what is taught in Romans 6 concerning our identification with Christ in His death, burial and resurrection.

When the Israelites marched through the Red Sea onto the victory side, the sea then closed in on the Egyptians who were following them. By this judgment of God, the power of the Egyptians over the Israelites was broken!

When a person receives Jesus Christ as Saviour, which is the application of Christ's shed blood, the individual is freed from the power of sin by his identification with the death and resurrection of Christ. So Israel's delivery from Egypt is a beautiful illustration of the believer's deliverance from the power of sin.

First Corinthians 10 is a significant chapter because it was written to believers and uses incidents from Israel's history to illustrate what is needed in believers' lives. This chapter was written to challenge believers to live victoriously. The chapter argues for a life that is lived on the basis of one's identification with Christ in His death, burial and resurrection. Galatians 2:20 expresses this identification: "I am crucified with Christ: nevertheless I live; yet not I, but Christ liveth in me: and the life which I now live in the flesh I live by the faith of the Son of God, who loved me, and gave himself for me." We have already seen this same truth expressed in Romans 6:4,5.

As we consider the parallels between Israel and the individual believer, the Passover represents salvation from the penalty, or condemnation, of sin. Deliverance through the Red Sea, however, represents deliverance from the power and slavery of sin.

It is important that those who know Jesus Christ as Saviour not only realize that they are saved from the condemnation of sin but that they are also saved from the power of sin—they no longer have to let sin dominate them. The Israelites were saved before they left their homes in Egypt, but their emancipation was not complete until the Red Sea took care of their enemies. As long as the Israelites were in enemy territory, they were subject to bondage.

Emancipation From Sin

Have you ever wondered why many people are still living in spiritual Egypt even though they have received Jesus Christ as Saviour? They are still living in defeat, although Christ has made it possible for them to live a life of victory. No believer will experience a life of victory until he realizes that he is identified with Christ.

God has provided a passport to victory, but it must be used, or relied on. It is not enough to know about it; we must live accordingly by appropriating this privilege in Christ. The recognition of our identification with Christ as set forth in Romans 6 leads to victory over sin.

Israel's march through the Red Sea serves as an example of complete emancipation from sin. God opened the sea, Israel marched through and Egypt marched after them. But when Israel stepped onto the victory side, the enemy was completely destroyed. The Israelites were then free from the slavery of Egypt.

In considering our relationship with Christ, we potentially died with Him when we trusted Him as Saviour. Also, since He had broken the power of the Devil (Heb. 2:14), we became identified with Him in victory. But although this victory is ours potentially, we must, by faith, act on what we know in order to make it ours experientially.

Romans 6:2-5 tells what actually took place from God's viewpoint. Verses 6-13 tell of the practical application as believers, by faith, appropriate what Christ accomplished in their behalf. It is important to realize that this is a position attained by faith. To be redeemed from death by the blood is great, but to remain in Egypt would be slavery, oppression and defeat. But that's where many Christians are living today—in spiritual Egypt.

Four key words in Romans 6 deserve special notice— know, reckon, yield and obey. When we know what has been accomplished in our behalf (v. 6) and reckon ourselves to be dead to sin, or accept it as a fact (v. 11), then we need to yield to the Lord (v. 13). Yielding is acting upon our faith. Our desire then will be to obey Him in everything (v. 17).

Pharaoh is an example of the enemy of the believer. After Pharaoh lost his slaves through blood redemption, he tried to recapture them in order to bring them under his domination. And after Satan loses people from his control when they receive Christ as Saviour, he also tries to bring them back under his domination. Satan will use all the devices he can in order to keep a believer in bondage so he will not be able to effectively serve Christ.

Reaction to the Enemy

Israel became terrified by the advances of the enemy and expressed fear in irrational ways. They accused Moses of false motives, thinking he had led them into the wilderness to die (Ex. 14:11), and spoke as if their salvation wasn't really worth it all (v. 12). They doubted that God could lead them to freedom, so they thought it was better to remain in slavery in Egypt.

It's also possible for new believers, like small children, to be frightened because they do not yet know God's power. But once a person tastes the life that God has for him, he will have no desire to return to what the world offers.

If you have trusted Jesus Christ as your Saviour, at what place in the Christian life are you? Are you a young Christian still looking back at the things of the world, or have you seen the full, rich life that is yours because of your personal relationship with Christ?

Like the disciples in the storm, we sometimes cry out, "Carest thou not that we perish?" (Mark 4:38) as if the Lord is unconcerned about us. The Israelites reacted in this way. God had brought them out of Egypt and through the Red Sea, but whenever they faced new trials, they thought surely the Lord did not care anything about them. This is why their faith needed to be tested—they needed to learn that God is sufficient for every need. They also needed to realize that they were not sufficient by themselves—and this is the lesson we need to learn.

Christians often quote Philippians 4:19: "My God shall supply all your need according to his riches in glory by Christ Jesus." But sometimes one wonders if they have really experienced the promise of this verse. God is sufficient to meet every need we have as we live according to His will.

Walking in accordance with God's will, however, sometimes means that we will go through severe testing (I Pet. 1:6,7). This testing is needed to give us a greater concept of who God is and what He wants to do in our lives. God also tests us so that we can learn what it is to be completely emancipated from the power of sin.

It is wonderful to be free from the power of sin and to be completely secure in the hand of God. The believer's security is seen clearly in the words of Jesus: "My sheep hear my voice, and I know them, and they follow me: and I give unto them eternal life; and they shall never perish, neither shall any man pluck them out of my hand. My Father, which gave them me, is greater than all; and no man is able to pluck them out of my Father's hand" (John 10:27-29). Our salvation is completely God's undertaking. This is why no one is able to pluck us out of His hand.

Romans 8:32 assures us, "He that spared not his own Son, but delivered him up for us all, how shall he not with him also freely give us all things?" And especially notice the triumphant statement of the following verses: "Who shall lay anything to the charge of God's elect? It is God that justifieth. Who is he that condemneth? It is Christ that died, yea rather, that is risen again, who is even at the right hand of God, who also maketh intercession for us" (vv. 33,34).

Our security in the Lord is also seen from Ephesians 1:13,14: "In whom ye also trusted, after that ye heard the word of truth, the gospel of your salvation: in whom also after that ye believed, ye were sealed with that holy Spirit of promise, which is the earnest of our inheritance until the redemption of the purchased possession, unto the praise of his glory."

Elements of Deliverance

In the plan of deliverance that God revealed to Israel, three distinct elements were mentioned in Exodus 14:13: "Moses said unto the people, Fear ye not, stand still, and see the salvation of the Lord."

First, notice the requirement of a right heart attitude—"fear ye not." Over and over again, God's Word instructs people not to fear. So often these instructions come, when, humanly speaking, there seems to be great reason to fear. Study the different people who were told not to fear, such as Abraham (Gen. 15:1), Joshua (Josh. 8:1), Gideon (Judg. 6:23), Daniel (Dan. 10:12) and the disciples (Luke 12:32).

God calls for fearless boldness such as was expressed by David: "Yea, though I walk through the valley of the shadow of death, I will fear no evil" (Ps. 23:4). Fearless boldness is also expressed in Psalm 118:6: "The Lord is on my side; I will not fear: what can man do unto me?"

As we consider how God worked with the nation of Israel, we learn many valuable principles concerning the way He works with the individual believer today. It is important that believers get a good foundation in these matters so that they can progress in the Christian life as God intends.

The Apostle Paul emphasized that the only foundation that can really be laid is Jesus Christ, and one needs to be careful how he builds on that foundation. Paul said, "According to the grace of God which is given unto me, as the wise masterbuilder, I have laid the foundation, and another buildeth thereon. But let every man take heed how he buildeth thereupon. For other foundation can no man lay than that is laid, which is Jesus Christ" (I Cor. 3:10,11).

If you have received Jesus Christ as your personal Saviour, then you have the proper foundation laid in your own life, but it is important that you build properly on that foundation in order to go on to spiritual maturity. That is why we are giving much attention to the spiritual lessons God taught Israel through Moses.

As Israel was fleeing from Egypt, the people became hemmed in on all four sides. They began to panic, for there was seemingly no way out of their dilemma. When they became convinced that the situation was hopeless, then God instructed the people through Moses: "Fear ye not, stand still, and see the salvation of the Lord, which he will shew to you to day: for the Egyptians whom ye have seen to day, ye shall see them again no more for ever" (Ex. 14:13). Notice those significant words, "Stand still, and see the salvation of the Lord." But notice that first of all God told them, "Fear ye not."

The Israelites were certainly in the valley of the shadow of death, and at this point they lacked the ability to say, "I will fear no evil," as David later wrote (Ps. 23:4).

The words of Moses to Israel, "Stand still" (Ex. 14:13), had the meaning of "Take your stand." Moses wanted the people to stand firm and wait on the Lord for deliverance.

God is determined to help those who will allow Him to do so. He is looking for those who are standing firm and have their eyes fixed on Him. The Bible says, "For the eyes of the Lord run to and fro throughout the whole earth, to shew himself strong in behalf of them whose heart is perfect toward him" (II Chron. 16:9).

The Example of Jehoshaphat

In this regard, Jehoshaphat's testimony is extremely encouraging. Jehoshaphat and his small army were surrounded and greatly outnumbered, but his confidence in God never waned. Jehoshaphat said, "O our God, wilt thou not judge them? For we have no might against this great company that cometh against us; neither know we what to do: but our eyes are upon thee" (II Chron. 20:12). And notice the way God responded to this kind of confidence in Him. He told Jehoshaphat, "Ye shall not need to fight in this battle: set yourselves, stand ye still, and see the salvation of the Lord with you, O Judah and Jerusalem: fear not, nor be dismayed; to morrow go out against them: for the Lord will be with you" (v. 17).

When we fix our eyes on the Lord and place our confidence in His ability to solve our problems, He will show Himself strong in our behalf. Notice, however, that God told Jehoshaphat and his army, "To morrow go out against them." On the one hand, we should realize the danger of going out in our own strength, or self-effort, but on the other hand we should beware of the other extreme—passivity. God nowhere condones the attitude which is expressed, or at least implied, by some believers who think they should remain idle and let the Lord do it all.

The Lord does not fight when the believer remains strictly passive. God promised victory to Jehoshaphat, but Jehoshaphat had the responsibility of leading his army out in order to participate in the victory God was going to give him.

As the believer goes into a spiritual battle, he needs to be constantly reminded that his confidence should never be in himself but in the Lord. As Isaiah 30:15 says, "In quietness and in confidence shall be your strength."

As Moses instructed the Israelites what to do in their desperate situation, he told them to stand still and "see the salvation of the Lord" (Ex. 14:13). The Israelites needed physical deliverance, but Moses was concerned that they also have spiritual sight to see the Lord work in their behalf. Although the circumstances and the enemy were against them, Moses did not want them to give an inch but to stand firm and see the salvation God was going to give them. In this way they would learn to know God as they had not known Him before.

It is important that the believer know God as far as salvation is concerned, but he should also know Him through seeing Him work in his daily life. In this regard, II Peter 1:3 contains tremendous truth: "According as his divine power hath given unto us all things that pertain unto life and godliness, through the knowledge of him that hath called us to glory and virtue." Note especially the words "unto life and godliness"; that is, eternal life and godly living.

Do you know Christ as your Saviour? If so, do you also know Him as the One who is able to provide all that you need for Christian living? When we get to know the Lord in this way, there's a quietness and confidence in our Christian walk.

Even when circumstances are against the believer, and even though unbelievers may be persecuting him, he can take confidence in Paul's words: "For our light affliction, which is but for a moment, worketh for us a far more exceeding and eternal weight of glory; while we look not at the things which are seen, but at the things which are not seen: for the things which are seen are temporal; but the things which are not seen are eternal" (II Cor. 4:17,18).

Although the Israelites had their eyes fixed on that which is temporal, Moses had his eyes fixed on that which is eternal—on God Himself. This is why Hebrews 11:27 says that Moses was "seeing him who is invisible." Moses had an understanding of God's program, and he wanted the people to have their spiritual eyes open to see it also. Moses wanted the people to realize that God would fight their battles if only they would stand firm and have confidence in Him.

This is why Moses told the people, "The Lord shall fight for you, and ye shall hold your peace" (Ex. 14:14). Moses made it clear to the people that the battle was the Lord's, not theirs.

The New Testament also reveals how the Lord fights for the believer. Galatians 5:17 says, "For the flesh lusteth against the Spirit, and the Spirit against the flesh: and these are contrary the one to the other: so that ye cannot do the things that ye would." This verse reveals that even though the sinful nature, or flesh, seeks to dominate the believer, the Holy Spirit strives against the flesh in behalf of the believer. Through the strength of the Holy Spirit, the believer can live above the pull of the flesh.

The Apostle Paul told of the conflict he had in his life as he sought to do what he knew was right and yet did not have the ability in himself to do it (Rom. 7:15-25). As he relied on the Holy Spirit, however, Paul was able to experience victory. This is why he said, "The law of the Spirit of life in Christ Jesus hath made me free from the law of sin and death. For what the law could not do, in that it was weak through the flesh, God sending his own Son in the likeness of sinful flesh, and for sin, condemned sin in the flesh: that the righteousness of the law might be fulfilled in us, who walk not after the flesh, but after the Spirit" (8:2-4).

The Holy Spirit frees the believer from the entanglements of the flesh. What a tremendous realization this is! God does all the fighting *for* the believer before he has become established in the faith. But even after he is more mature, the Holy Spirit does the fighting *through* the believer.

Actively Claiming Victory

Even though the Israelites were told to "stand still" (Ex. 14:13), God also told them to "go forward" (v. 15). This reveals that the "stand still" did not mean they were to be completely passive; rather, they were to stand firm and put confidence in the Lord for the victory He could and would give them as they moved ahead. It is important to realize that God gives us the victory He promises only as we move ahead to take it. A key verse on this subject is Joshua 1:3. God had promised the Israelites the land, but He told Joshua, "Every place that the sole of your foot shall tread upon, that have I given unto you, as I said unto Moses." Although the Lord had promised the land to the Israelites, they needed to move in, by faith, and take it.

God makes the victory available to us, but He expects us to be obedient in moving forward and taking the victory.

Before the command was given by God to the Israelites concerning moving forward, He promised them that they would not see the Egyptians any more forever (Ex. 14:13). The invisible God promised them the victory before the people were commanded to go forward and take the victory. They knew the promise, and they were to move ahead according to it and claim it.

In Israel's case, we see that God leads forward, not backward. And in their situation, God did not even lead around but through. God told Moses, "But lift thou up thy rod, and stretch out thine hand over the sea, and divide it: and the children of Israel shall go on dry ground through the midst of the sea" (v. 16). Although, humanly speaking, they could see no way out, God promised to take them through the barrier before them.

Moses' Rod

As the Lord was instructing Moses concerning opening the Red Sea, He told him, "Lift thou up thy rod, and stretch out thine hand" (Ex. 14:16). What a helpless, hopeless action this would normally be! There was no magical power in Moses' rod. He was about as helpless in this situation as was the lame man to whom Jesus said, "Take up thy bed, and walk" (John 5:11). But God always gives the ability to do what He commands. This was true with the Israelites and with the people Jesus healed, and it is true with us. We need to learn to live one day at a time, even one step at a time. As we take one step, depending on God, He will provide the strength we need, and then we will be ready for the next step.

God was trying to teach Israel valuable lessons so the people would be ready to meet the obstacles they would face in the future. They had to fight battles on the way to Canaan, the Jordan River had to be crossed and Jericho had to be taken—but in each case God would be with them and enable them to have victory if they would only trust Him. God would go before them as a good shepherd goes before his sheep (John 10:4,27); their responsibility was to follow Him.

Not only did God command the Israelites to go forward but He also instructed them how to go forward. He told Moses to divide the sea by taking his rod and stretching out his hand over the sea so the Israelites could go through on dry ground (Ex. 14:16). The rod Moses had was that of a shepherd, but yielded to God, it was the rod of God. God did many miracles with that rod in the hand of Moses as he was obedient and used it to God's glory.

Humanly speaking, it was foolish to think that Moses could divide the Red Sea with the rod he held in his hand. However, we must not forget the principle that God uses what the world considers foolish to demonstrate the foolishness of what the world considers wise (I Cor. 1:26-28). The reason God works this way is so that "no flesh should glory in his presence" (v. 29) and to teach us the lesson of verse 31: "He that glorieth, let him glory in the Lord."

Escape for Israel; Destruction for Egypt

God was not yet through with the Egyptians. He told Moses, "Behold, I will harden the hearts of the Egyptians, and they shall follow them: and I will get me honour upon Pharaoh, and upon all his host, upon his chariots, and upon his horsemen" (Ex. 14:17).

God allowed Pharaoh and his army to follow Israel so that in one event Israel was saved and Egypt was destroyed. The opening of the Red Sea was the means of escape for the Israelites, but it was the means of destruction for the power of Egypt.

So also, God allowed Satan to stir up anger against the Lord Jesus Christ in order to have Jesus crucified. But the death of Jesus Christ not only provided salvation for all who would believe in Him, it also destroyed Satan's power (Col. 2:15; Heb. 2:14).

Notice God's purpose for allowing the Egyptians to pursue the Israelites: "The Egyptians shall know that I am the Lord, when I have gotten me honour upon Pharaoh, upon his chariots, and upon his horsemen" (Ex. 14:18). After the incident of the Red Sea there would be no doubt that God had acted in behalf of His people and that He had brought to nothing the greatest power on earth.

The Bible also reveals that God brought glory to Himself even through the death of Jesus Christ. Philippians 2:9-11 says, "Wherefore God hath highly exalted him, and given him a name which is above every name: that at the name of Jesus every knee should bow, of things in heaven, and things in earth, and things under the earth; and that every tongue should confess that Jesus Christ is Lord, to the glory of God the Father." Even those who reject Jesus Christ as Saviour will someday have to acknowledge that He is Lord of all.

This reveals how important it is that each person seriously consider his relationship with Jesus Christ and receive Him as Saviour and Lord before it is eternally too late.

As the Egyptians pursued the Israelites, "the angel of God, which went before the camp of Israel, removed and went behind them; and the pillar of the cloud went from before their face, and stood behind them: and it came between the camp of the Egyptians and the camp of Israel; and it was a cloud and darkness to them, but it gave light by night to these: so that the one came not near the other all the night" (Ex. 14:19,20).

God had already promised Israel the victory; now He provided protection for them. In Egypt God had provided the lamb to save the Israelites from death when He passed over the land; now He provided a cloud to protect them from death by the Egyptians.

This reveals the principle that God not only provides for salvation but also for daily living. This is clearly stated in Romans 5:8-10: "But God commendeth his love toward us, in that, while we were yet sinners, Christ died for us. Much more then, being now justified by his blood, we shall be saved from wrath through him. For if, when we were enemies, we were reconciled to God by the death of his Son, much more, being reconciled, we shall be saved by his life." If God provided what we needed in salvation, surely we can expect Him to provide what we need to bring glory to Him in our daily lives.

God and Circumstances

The Israelites often made the mistake of interpreting God in the light of their circumstances, and most believers have this same tendency today. But just as God caused a cloud to move between the Israelites and the Egyptians, so God puts Himself between the believer and circumstances.

As adverse situations develop in our lives, we should not feel defeat; rather, we should ask ourselves what God wants to accomplish in our lives through the circumstances. We must fix our spiritual eyes on God and realize that He is in control of circumstances. When we recognize this, we will not be defeated by adverse situations; we will respond positively to them and try to discover what God has in them for us.

The Bible records an incident which emphasizes the different way people respond to circumstances. As the Israelites were on their way to Canaan, they came to Kadesh-barnea where 12 men were sent into Canaan to spy out the land (Num. 13). Ten of the men returned with a report that revealed they were looking only at the circumstances and not at God. As a result, their recommendation was, "We be not able to go up against the people; for they are stronger than we" (v. 31). But two of the spies, Joshua and Caleb, had their eyes fixed on God rather than on the circumstances. Caleb's recommendation was, "Let us go up at once, and possess it; for we are well able to overcome it" (v. 30).

When one concentrates on the circumstances, God becomes small; when one concentrates on God, the circumstances become small. This is what we need to realize, and this is what Israel needed to realize as they were fleeing from the Egyptians.

The Bible reveals that it was God, not Israel, who actually fought the Egyptians. Exodus 14:24,25 says, "And it came to pass, that in the morning watch the Lord looked unto the host of the Egyptians through the pillar of fire and of the cloud, and troubled the host of the Egyptians, and took off their chariot wheels, that they drave them heavily: so that the Egyptians said, Let us flee from the face of Israel; for the Lord fighteth for them against the Egyptians." What a statement! Even the unbelieving Egyptians realized God was fighting against them.

Just as God provided protection for the Israelites, so also He provides protection for the individual believer. This does not mean that we will always be delivered from testings or difficult circumstances, but it means that God will be with us and fight for us in those situations. Ephesians 1:13,14 assures believers, "Ye were sealed with that holy Spirit of promise, which is the earnest of our inheritance until the redemption of the purchased possession, unto the praise of his glory." Ephesians 4:30 tells us we are sealed with the Holy Spirit "unto the day of redemption." And the Lord assures the believer, "I will never leave thee, nor forsake thee" (Heb. 13:5). With promises like these there is no reason for us to fear circumstances.

Note another way the Lord protected Israel: "The children of Israel went into the midst of the sea upon the dry ground: and the waters were a wall unto them on their right hand, and on their left" (Ex. 14:22). There was no way the enemy could get to them—a cloud was between them and the enemy, and the walls of water protected them on each side. And while they were protected from the sides and from the rear, the Israelites were able to go ahead in full light as God led the way.

The water of the Red Sea had symbolized death to the Israelites, but now it had no power over them. Instead, it was actually a defense for them. The very sea which they had so feared had now become their means of deliverance! And that which became salvation for the Israelites became death to their enemy.

God Fights the Enemy

Exodus 14:24,25 reveals how God hindered the enemy of the Israelites. He "troubled the host of the Egyptians, and took off their chariot wheels, that they drave them heavily: so that the Egyptians said, Let us flee from the face of Israel; for the Lord fighteth for them against the Egyptians."

God's resistance of Israel's enemy is a reminder of the way He is resisting Satan's program right now. God is preventing Satan from accomplishing his desires with us, because He is restraining sin by means of the Holy Spirit actively working in the lives of believers. Second Thessalonians 2:6,7 tells of this restraining work: "And you know what restrains him now, so that in his time he may be revealed. For the mystery of lawlessness is already at work; only he who now restrains will do so until he is taken out of the way" (NASB). The Holy Spirit, working through believers, will restrain sin until the Rapture of the Church, when believers will be removed from earth to heaven. After this, the Holy Spirit will continue His work on earth in much the same way that He did before Pentecost.

After the Rapture of the Church the entire earth will experience a seven-year period of tribulation. How wonderful it is to realize that God protects His own. The Bible says, "No weapon that is formed against thee shall prosper; and

every tongue that shall rise against thee in judgment thou
shalt condemn. This is the heritage of the servants of the
Lord, and their righteousness is of me, saith the Lord" (Isa.
54:17).

Psalm 91 also assures the believer of the protective hand
of the Lord. "He who dwells in the shelter of the Most High
will abide in the shadow of the Almighty. I will say to the
Lord, 'My refuge and my fortress, my God, in whom I trust!'
For it is He who delivers you from the snare of the trapper,
and from the deadly pestilence. He will cover you with His
pinions, and under His wings you may seek refuge; His faithfulness is a shield and bulwark. You will not be afraid of the
terror by night, or of the arrow that flies by day" (vv. 1-5,
NASB).

As the believer looks around him today and sees many
things that might cause him to be frightened, he is instructed
by the Lord through His Word not to be afraid because God
will be with him no matter what happens. Psalm 91 also says,
"A thousand may fall at your side, and ten thousand at your
right hand; but it shall not approach you. You will only look
on with your eyes, and see the recompense of the wicked.
For you have made the Lord, my refuge, even the Most High,
your dwelling place. No evil will befall you, nor will any
plague come near your tent. . . . Because he has loved Me,
therefore I will deliver him; I will set him securely on high,
because he has known My name. He will call upon Me, and I
will answer him; I will be with him in trouble; I will rescue
him, and honor him. With a long life I will satisfy him, and
let him behold My salvation" (vv. 7-10, 14-16, NASB).

As God did all of the fighting and protecting of the
Israelites, the result was the overthrow of Egypt. "Moses
stretched forth his hand over the sea, and the sea returned to
his strength when the morning appeared; and the Egyptians
fled against it; and the Lord overthrew the Egyptians in the
midst of the sea. And the waters returned, and covered the
chariots, and the horsemen, and all the host of Pharaoh that
came into the sea after them; there remained not so much as
one of them" (Ex. 14:27,28).

Egypt's chief strength and glory was its king and its army.
While the Egyptians had previously suffered great judgment,
the triumphant army had not been weakened in its power.

But God completely overthrew Egypt and broke its power once and for all. As a nation, Egypt continued to exist, but it was never again such a mighty world power.

Just as Egypt's power to hold Israel captive and enslave God's people was broken, so also Satan's power to enslave was broken by the death of the Lord Jesus Christ. Hebrews 2:14 says, "Forasmuch then as the children are partakers of flesh and blood, he [Jesus Christ] also himself likewise took part of the same; that through death he might destroy him that had the power of death, that is, the devil." (See also Col. 2:15.)

As the power of Egypt over the Israelites was broken, so also the power of sin over the believer was broken by Christ's death. Romans 8:3 says, "For what the law could not do, in that it was weak through the flesh, God sending his own Son in the likeness of sinful flesh, and for sin, condemned sin in the flesh."

Israel's Complete Emancipation

The final verses of Exodus 14 reveal that the emancipation of Israel was completed: "But the children of Israel walked upon dry land in the midst of the sea; and the waters were a wall unto them on their right hand, and on their left. Thus the Lord saved Israel that day out of the hand of the Egyptians; and Israel saw the Egyptians dead upon the sea shore. And Israel saw that great work which the Lord did upon the Egyptians: and the people feared the Lord, and believed the Lord, and his servant Moses" (vv. 29-31).

The dead bodies of the Egyptians on the seashore were the evidence of Israel's complete emancipation. This sight brought great fear on Israel; they believed God, and Moses was completely vindicated in their eyes. They saw that their redemption was completely of God, working through Moses after they had shed the blood of the lamb and applied it to their doorposts. So also, our redemption is completely of God through a Person—Jesus Christ. Only as we apply His shed blood by receiving Him as Saviour can we benefit from what He accomplished for us on the cross. Just as Israel had complete emancipation from the power of Egypt and its slavery, so we who trust Christ are completely emancipated from Satan's power to enslave us in sin.

It is especially important that a believer realize the total emancipation God has provided for him. The Christian who does not realize this will not progress in the Christian life as God intends. Having accepted the total victory that God has accomplished for us, we then need to walk, or live, on the basis of it.

The incident of God delivering Israel through the Red Sea is specifically referred to in I Corinthians 10:1,2: "Moreover, brethren, I would not that ye should be ignorant, how that all our fathers were under the cloud, and all passed through the sea; and were all baptized unto Moses in the cloud and in the sea." Verse 11 says, "Now all these things happened unto them for ensamples [examples]: and they are written for our admonition, upon whom the ends of the world are come." The things that happened to Israel were literally types in that they prefigure that which takes place in an individual believer's life.

The crossing of the Red Sea indicates that God made a way through death for His people. Thus, the Red Sea was the boundary line of the Egyptians' power over the Israelites. As a parallel, Christ's death on the cross marks the boundary line of Satan's power over those who trust in Christ.

Death and Resurrection

It is important to realize that there is resurrection as well as death in Christ. The Bible says, "For if we have been planted together in the likeness of his death, we shall be also in the likeness of his resurrection" (Rom. 6:5).

The person who has received Jesus Christ as Saviour has participated in His death, and he has also participated in His resurrection—believers have been raised to sit together with Christ in the heavenlies (Eph. 2:5,6).

After God's judgment on the Egyptians at the Red Sea, Israel was dead to Egypt and all that was connected to it. Egypt no longer had any power over the Israelites. The cloud and the sea were to the Israelites what the cross and the grave of Christ are to us. The cloud gave them security from the enemy; the sea separated them from Egypt. The cross of

Christ shields us from that which is against us; the grave, the place of death, reveals that in Christ we are dead to the world. We stand on heaven's side, or the resurrection side, of the empty tomb of Jesus.

After the Israelites had passed through the Red Sea, the waters of death flowed between them and the place of bondage, cutting them off from Egypt's power. The Israelites were on resurrection ground and were to begin their journey through the wilderness to taste of the heavenly manna and water from the spiritual rock. All of this and more the Israelites were to benefit from as they marched toward the land of rest. But it took them a long time to reach the place of their destination. So also, it takes many Christians a long time to recognize that they have been separated from bondage and that they are actually free to do the will of God.

Just as the crossing of the Red Sea completed the deliverance of Israel from Egypt in order that they could begin their journey toward the Promised Land, so also when a person trusts Christ and has complete salvation, he is to progress in his Christian walk.

As the Israelites were identified with Moses in the Red Sea (I Cor. 10:2), so the believer is united with Christ in His death and resurrection. Paul alluded to this union with Christ when he said, "I am crucified with Christ: nevertheless I live; yet not I, but Christ liveth in me: and the life which I now live in the flesh I live by the faith of the Son of God, who loved me, and gave himself for me" (Gal. 2:20). (See also Rom. 6:5 and Eph. 2:5,6.)

The crossing of both the Red Sea and the Jordan River illustrate what was accomplished for the believer in the death of Christ. At the Red Sea there was separation from Egypt; at the Jordan River there was an entering into the place of rest. The place of rest for the believer is referred to in Hebrews 4:9,10: "There remaineth therefore a rest to the people of God. For he that is entered into his rest, he also hath ceased from his own works, as God did from his."

For the believer the death of Christ not only separates him from this present evil world, but it also makes him spiritually alive and seats him with Christ. What a glorious truth this is! We are on the resurrection side. We have much more than the forgiveness of sin; we have been associated with the risen Christ so that we may be united with Him forever and live the heavenly life. He who was dead is now alive! And this same Jesus indwells the bodies of believers in order to live His life in them (I Cor. 6:19,20). What a glorious privilege is ours!

Completed Promises of God

The fact that God was able to bring the Israelites out of Egypt was an assurance that He also had the ability to bring them into the land. This is precisely what He had promised the Israelites. God had said, "I will bring you out from under the burdens of the Egyptians" (Ex. 6:6). But He had also promised, "I will bring you in unto the land" (v. 8).

So also, God has not only redeemed us, but He also has the ability to complete the work He has begun. "Being confident of this very thing, that he which hath begun a good work in you will perform it until the day of Jesus Christ" (Phil. 1:6).

In order that we might have an indication that God is going to complete His work, He has given us the Holy Spirit. Paul reminded the Ephesian believers, "In whom ye also trusted, after that ye heard the word of truth, the gospel of your salvation: in whom also after that ye believed, ye were sealed with that holy Spirit of promise, which is the earnest of our inheritance until the redemption of the purchased possession, unto the praise of his glory" (Eph. 1:13,14).

It is wonderful to know that we are sealed with the Holy Spirit "unto the day of redemption" (4:30). God has given the Holy Spirit to the believer as an earnest, or an evidence, that He will complete what He has promised.

God has made available to us the same power that raised Jesus Christ from the dead. The Apostle Paul was concerned that all believers might know "what is the exceeding greatness of his power to us-ward who believe, according to the working of his mighty power, which he wrought in Christ, when he raised him from the dead, and set him at his own right hand in the heavenly places, far above all principality, and power, and might, and dominion, and every name that is named, not only in this world, but also in that which is to come" (1:19-21).

Someday those of us who know Jesus Christ as Saviour will be displayed as trophies of His grace, as is indicated in Ephesians 2:6,7: "And hath raised us up together, and made us sit together in heavenly places in Christ Jesus: that in the ages to come he might shew the exceeding riches of his grace in his kindness toward us through Christ Jesus."

No wonder the Bible says that Jesus Christ "is able also to save them to the uttermost that come unto God by him" (Heb. 7:25). The reason He is able to save us to the uttermost is seen in the last phrase of this same verse: "Seeing he ever liveth to make intercession for them."

Having begun the work of salvation, God is not going to let us down before it is completed. God has made available to us all that we need for salvation and also for the Christian life. That is why the Bible says, "We know that all things work together for good to them that love God, to them who are the called according to his purpose" (Rom. 8:28). This enables us to be "more than conquerors through him that loved us" (v. 37). What tremendous encouragement this is to walk in the way He has so richly provided in Christ!

Chapter 8

The Song of Assurance and Praise

Exodus 14 reveals a people under the pressure of their circumstances—self was extremely prominent. Exodus 15 reveals a people with pressures removed—self was forgotten.

A nation of slaves, fleeing from their masters, had suddenly become a nation of free men. They stood on the shores of a new land, completely emancipated from their slave owners. The proud nation of Egypt, which for generations had inflicted indescribable grief on them, had suffered a humiliation so great that they would never completely recover from it.

Praise and Worship

As the early morning light broke, the Israelites stood on the seashore and viewed the dead bodies of their enemies. As the people of God realized the glorious victory and release they had just experienced, they burst into a song of extraordinary praise and worship to God.

In the Israelites' song recorded in Exodus 15, the word "Lord" occurs 11 times, and various personal pronouns referring to Him occur more than 30 times. So it is clear that the song was sung *to* Him and *about* Him. All the honors of the victory were reverently laid at His feet.

In this song of assurance and praise, Moses is not mentioned once. This indicates that the Israelites now had complete confidence in the trustworthiness of God. The last verse of Exodus 14 says that the people "believed the Lord, and his servant Moses" (v. 31), but Moses is not mentioned in the song. Those who really understand spiritual realities

69

know they should focus attention on the Lord, not on the servant.

When self is forgotten and our eyes are turned totally to the Lord, praise must come forth. The normal result of worship is praise. If we are not expressing praise to the Lord and about the Lord, the indication is that we are not really occupied with the Person of Christ as we ought to be.

Each believer would do well to ask himself, What does the indwelling Christ really mean to me? To some, He is only theology. But He is to be much more than that to the believer; He is an inner, spiritual, living experience and reality. When we have our eyes opened to Christ's great work for us and in us through our identification in His death, burial and resurrection, we will gladly praise Him.

Although every believer has eternal life in Christ (I John 5:12), Christ wants to be much more than salvation to us. He wants us to be gripped with the reality of His indwelling and the outworking of His life in us. Do you experientially know the reality of His abiding, indwelling presence and the outworking of His life?

The Lord Jesus Christ is everything to the believer—"Christ in you, the hope of glory" (Col. 1:27). Knowing the reality of that caused the Apostle Paul to say, "Whereunto I also labour, striving according to his working, which worketh in me mightily" (v. 29). (See also Gal. 2:20.) As we recognize the reality of Christ's continued presence and of His working in us, our faith is strengthened. This is also the basis for spiritual victory.

The Lord Jesus Christ will not fail us; He will see us through to the end (see Rom. 8:29,30,32,35-39; Phil. 1:6). However, we must learn to believe God even when circumstances are against us. Israel expressed such confidence as they saw themselves as victors over all their enemies. In their song of assurance and praise, it is evident that the Israelites realized the victory they had just experienced was an indication of victory that would be theirs in the future. They believed all of God's promises listed in Exodus 6:6-8, from emancipation to the entering of Canaan.

Notice some of the great words of their song: "Who is like Thee among the gods, O Lord? Who is like Thee, majestic in holiness, awesome in praises, working wonders? Thou didst stretch out Thy right hand, the earth swallowed them. In Thy lovingkindness Thou hast led the people whom Thou hast redeemed; in Thy strength Thou has guided them to Thy holy habitation. The peoples have heard, they tremble; anguish has gripped the inhabitants of Philistia. Then the chiefs of Edom were dismayed; the leaders of Moab, trembling grips them; all the inhabitants of Canaan have melted away. Terror and dread fall upon them; by the greatness of Thine arm they are motionless as stone; until Thy people pass over, O Lord, until the people pass over whom Thou hast purchased. Thou wilt bring them and plant them in the mountain of Thine inheritance, the place, O Lord, which Thou hast made for Thy dwelling, the sanctuary, O Lord, which Thy hands have established. The Lord shall reign forever and ever" (15:11-18, NASB).

Confidence for the Future

Although the Israelites were right in their viewpoint at this time, they faltered later when tests came. But even though the Israelites faltered and failed, God remained true to His promises. It is interesting to note, however, that the Israelites sang their victory song even before they took the first step into the wilderness. They were aware of God's promises, so at this time they were confident of victory even though they later faltered.

God has also made many promises to the believer today (see Rom. 8:38,39; Eph. 1:13,14; I Pet. 1:4-7). We, too, need to be assured of the trustworthiness of God if we are to progress in the Christian life by growing to spiritual maturity. How wonderful it is to recognize that God knows the end as well as the beginning. So we may, like Israel, sing the song of victory even before we take the first step into the wilderness of future experiences in our daily walk.

Having confidence in God even before one meets obstacles is what faith is all about. Hebrews 11 tells of many heroes of the faith who had an unshakable confidence in the trustworthiness of God.

The fact that Israel experienced many failures later as they were tested is a reminder to us that the hope and joy we experience in Christ at the height of some previous experience often lasts only until He permits another test to strike us. How important it is, therefore, that we have our spiritual eyes fixed on Christ Himself, not on a past experience.

As we have complete confidence in Christ, we will be able to say with the Apostle Paul, "I know whom I have believed, and am persuaded that he is able to keep that which I have committed unto him against that day" (II Tim. 1:12).

Chapter 9

Entering the Desert Experience

Moses was a person of tremendous faith. He demonstrated this by taking about three million people into a desert where there was no water, no food, no shelter, no roads—nothing. Yet he had confidence that God could and would sustain them physically since He had ordered them to go into the desert.

Moses knew the desert well, for he had spent 40 years there learning spiritual lessons from God before he was commissioned to return to Egypt to lead the Israelites out. Of course, the object of Moses' faith was much more important than the amount or greatness of his faith. To learn this is to learn one of the greatest lessons of all—our faith must not be in our faith, it must be in God.

What concept of God do you have? Is He a little God as far as you are concerned? Does He have only a small amount of power? Or is He a great God to you? Does He have the ability to accomplish whatever He pleases? Only when you recognize Him as all-powerful and all-wise will you be able to have the song of assurance and praise that Moses and the Israelites had.

Dependent on God's Provision

The Israelites had been redeemed by blood from the judgment that fell on Egypt, and they had been redeemed by the power of God from the slavery of Egypt. But now they needed to learn how to walk in God's path.

So, too, when a person today receives Jesus Christ as Saviour and is delivered from the condemnation and power of sin, he needs to learn how to walk with God in the way He leads.

Just as Israel needed a training period, so every believer today needs a training period. In the wilderness the Israelites were shut out from the world around them and were completely alone with God—they had to depend on Him for everything. The training they received was to help them see the futility of the self-life.

Everyone, because of their sinful nature, is basically selfish. Only when a person receives Jesus Christ as Saviour is he given a new perspective so that he can have a genuine concern for others. But sometimes even a believer needs to go through difficult tests in order to learn not to rely on self. That is what happened to Israel—God brought tests into their lives to teach them to rely on Him for everything.

The Bible records: "So Moses brought Israel from the Red sea, and they went out into the wilderness of Shur; and they went three days in the wilderness, and found no water" (Ex. 15:22). Imagine—about three million people and no water! But this was precisely the kind of predicament God wanted Israel to experience so they would have no alternative but to trust Him completely. God was for the nation, not against it, so they really had no reason to fear as long as they were obedient to Him.

The spiritual lessons the Israelites had learned so far were associated with birth and babyhood experiences. Now that they were a free people, although still very much under God's watchful care, they were to experientially grow in stature so that as mature people they might enter, conquer and possess the Promised Land. At this point, the Israelites weren't ready for what was coming in Canaan, so God had to train them and prepare them for that crucial time.

The Israelites had learned from experience that God alone had accomplished their redemption and emancipation from Egypt. They simply accepted what God had done for them. During the next two years of Israel's history, the people were to see a demonstration of God's provision for their every need. This was a fulfillment of what God had promised through Moses: "I will take you to me for a people, and I will be to you a God: and ye shall know that I am the

Lord your God, which bringeth you out from under the burdens of the Egyptians" (6:7).

The next two years were to be filled with many learning experiences for the Israelites. As far as they knew at the time they fled from Egypt, they would be in the land of Canaan within a few weeks. But additional time was needed in order to teach them valuable spiritual lessons. They were taught to follow, to believe and to obey God. God could not take them any faster through these experiences because it took them so long to learn the lessons.

The Israelites had already become acquainted with the cloud which was God's visible means of leadership, light and protection. They were soon to experience God's providing manna, meat, water and many other necessities for their journey.

God provided for the Israelites because of the nation's relationship to Him. So, too, all that is provided for the individual believer is due to his perfect position in Christ. Those who know Christ as Saviour need to seriously consider and establish in their minds the significance of this position.

Jesus said, "He that heareth my word, and believeth on him that sent me, hath everlasting life, and shall not come into condemnation; but is passed from death unto life" (John 5:24). The person who knows Christ as Saviour can also claim the promise of Romans 8:1: "There is therefore now no condemnation to them which are in Christ Jesus." Ephesians 1:13,14 tells the believer that the Holy Spirit has been given to him as an earnest, or pledge, that God will complete what He has begun. Philippians 1:6 specifically states this: "Being confident of this very thing, that he which hath begun a good work in you will perform it until the day of Jesus Christ."

The believer is not to trust in himself. He is to realize that all of his sufficiency is found in Jesus Christ. As the Apostle Paul said, "Not that we are sufficient of ourselves to think any thing as of ourselves; but our sufficiency is of God" (II Cor. 3:5). The believer's completeness in Christ is noted in Colossians 2:9,10: "For in him dwelleth all the fulness of the Godhead bodily. And ye are complete in him, which is the head of all principality and power." How wonderful it is to realize that God has provided us with "all things that pertain unto life and godliness" (II Pet. 1:3). We receive a new nature when we accept Jesus Christ as Saviour. Because of this we even have a change in our desires—we want to please Him and to serve Him rather than desiring to please ourselves and to serve sin.

Progressing to Maturity

The way a believer is to live the Christian life is stated in Colossians 2:6: "As ye have therefore received Christ Jesus the Lord, so walk ye in him." A person receives Christ as Saviour by grace through faith (Eph. 2:8), so he is to live by the same principle. No one is able to work for his salvation, so we do not go on to spiritual maturity by works.

We become spiritually mature as we learn to exercise faith in God for every step of the way. Colossians 2:7 reveals that we are to be "rooted and built up in him, and stablished in the faith, as ye have been taught, abounding therein with thanksgiving." As we learn more about God and His way and have a greater confidence in Him and His provisions for us, we, too, will be "rooted and built up in him."

Someone might ask, How do we become spiritually mature? A partial answer is found in Hebrews 5:12-14. Verses 12,13 say, "For when for the time ye ought to be teachers, ye have need that one teach you again which be the first principles of the oracles of God; and are become such as have need of milk, and not of strong meat. For every one that useth milk is unskilful in the word of righteousness: for he is a babe." But how does a believer develop to the point that he is able to take strong meat? The answer is in verse 14: "But strong meat belongeth to them that are of full age, even those who by reason of use have their senses exercised to discern both good and evil." We become spiritually mature as we exercise our spiritual senses. When we apply the Word of God to daily life situations, the result will be spiritual growth.

Having told the Hebrew Christians of the need for spiritual maturity and how to accomplish it, the writer of Hebrews said, "Therefore leaving the principles of the doctrine of Christ, let us go on unto perfection [maturity]; not laying again the foundation of repentance from dead works, and of faith toward God, of the doctrine of baptisms, and of laying on of hands, and of resurrection of the dead, and of eternal judgment" (6:1,2). In other words, we are to leave the foundational things and go on to maturity. Notice that we are not to lay again the foundation but to build upon it as we go on to maturity.

The Apostle Paul said, "For other foundation can no man lay than that is laid, which is Jesus Christ" (I Cor. 3:11). When a person receives Jesus Christ as Saviour, the true foundation has been laid in his life. He never again needs to lay the foundation, but he does need to build on that foundation with quality materials, as indicated by Paul in verses 12-15. Those who have built with "gold, silver, precious stones" will be rewarded, but there will be no reward for those who have built with "wood, hay, stubble."

The Israelites had their foundation laid when they were delivered from Egypt by means of the Passover and when the nation was emancipated from Egypt's slavery as it passed through the Red Sea. These experiences never needed to be repeated, but it was important that the people go on in their walk with God and build on the foundation that had been laid.

It is important for those who know Jesus Christ as Saviour to know about the perfect position they have in Him. But it is also important that they learn to apply all the strength that is available as a result of their union with Him. This is what Paul referred to when he said, "I am crucified with Christ: nevertheless I live; yet not I, but Christ liveth in me" (Gal. 2:20). By faith we are to apply, or appropriate, the strength of God made available to us by putting on the whole armor of God (Eph. 6:10-13).

The road ahead for the three million Israelites in a barren desert was a human impossibility. However, God was about to demonstrate His power in a way which the world had never seen before.

So, too, it is impossible to live the Christian life in this world of sin in the power of human strength alone. This is why the Lord Jesus told us: "Abide in me, and I in you. As the branch cannot bear fruit of itself, except it abide in the vine; no more can ye, except ye abide in me. I am the vine, ye are the branches: he that abideth in me, and I in him, the same bringeth forth much fruit: for without me ye can do nothing" (John 15:4,5).

Just as the Israelites had to be brought to the end of themselves, so every believer must have the same experience. In Romans 7 Paul expressed how he came to the end of himself, and in Romans 8 he sounded the glorious note of having found victory through the Holy Spirit's strength which was made available to him as he, by faith, appropriated what he needed.

Israel's Needs Supplied

In the desert Israel was completely shut in to God. The people had to depend on God to supply everything through His man, Moses. Moses was their well-trained and mature leader who was competent to help them know God and His way intimately. We can begin to understand why God took so much time in training Moses—there was an overwhelming task ahead of him. God had to prepare Moses so he would not give in to the Israelites under pressure. Moses' faith had to be deeply rooted in God so he would have complete confidence in God, even in the face of seeming impossibility. Moses did not know how or where God was going to lead or what God was going to do, but he was sure God knew what He was doing. This was the tremendous confidence Moses had in God.

God provided leadership for the Israelites in the person of Moses. The believer today has also been given a leader—the Holy Spirit. Before Jesus ascended to heaven, He told His disciples, "I will pray the Father, and he shall give you another Comforter, that he may abide with you for ever; even the Spirit of truth; whom the world cannot receive, because it seeth him not, neither knoweth him: but ye know him; for he dwelleth with you, and shall be in you" (John 14:16,17).

According to Hebrews 7:25 and 8:1 Jesus Christ is enthroned and is interceding for us, yet the life and power that He is and has indwells us by means of the Holy Spirit. When Jesus Christ was on earth, He lived a perfect life through the power of the Holy Spirit. Now, by the same Holy Spirit, the life of Jesus Christ is available to us and is produced in us. Our strength and ability is derived from Jesus Christ by means of the Holy Spirit.

In the desert Israel had no water or food; these things were supplied only by direct miracles of God. This was the way that God chose to prove Himself to Israel. Israel found no natural springs in the desert to quench their thirst; they had to rely totally on God to satisfy their needs.

So, too, the basic needs of the Christian cannot be supplied by the world. Only God can provide that which deeply satisfies the spiritual needs of the believer. Just as Israel found no natural springs in the desert to satisfy their thirst, so the believer finds no earthly springs that can satisfy his spiritual thirst. The Israelites were not desert people—they were not *of* the desert, they were just passing through. So also the believer is not of this world, he is only passing through.

This reminds us of Abraham, of whom it was said, "By faith he sojourned in the land of promise, as in a strange country, dwelling in tabernacles [tents] with Isaac and Jacob, the heirs with him of the same promise: for he looked for a city which hath foundations, whose builder and maker is God" (Heb. 11:9,10).

Philippians 3:20 reveals that believers are actually citizens of the heavenly country: "For our conversation [citizenship] is in heaven; from whence also we look for the Saviour, the Lord Jesus Christ." In encouraging Christians to witness concerning the crucifixion, Hebrews 13:13,14 says, "Let us go forth therefore unto him without the camp, bearing his reproach. For here have we no continuing city, but we seek one to come." The testimony of the songwriter should be the testimony of every Christian: "This world is not my home, I'm just a-passing through."

It is almost impossible to comprehend all that would be involved in taking care of the needs of the Israelites in the desert. A Christian military officer once stationed in that area of the world calculated that it would take approximately 4000 tons of food a day to feed the three million Israelites. He also calculated that it would take two freight trains, each a mile long, to haul that amount of food. He made many other interesting calculations, but the important thing to realize is that there was no way, humanly speaking, that the needs of the Israelites could be taken care of.

The Purpose of Testing

Exodus 15:22 states that the Israelites started on their journey through the wilderness after passing through the Red Sea. They had been redeemed by blood from condemnation; they had been redeemed by the power of God from the slavery of the Egyptians. They probably expected that they would have a smooth journey from there on. Perhaps they thought, Aren't we the chosen people of God? Surely God is obligated to bring us into the Promised Land without more difficulty. But immediately after their song of assurance and praise for what God had done, they experienced severe testing. They "found no water" (v. 22).

This often happens—after a time of victory comes a time of testing. We see this principle even in the life of the Lord Jesus Christ. At His baptism there was the glorious announcement: "This is my beloved Son, in whom I am well pleased" (Matt. 3:17). But immediately afterward came the testing from Satan (4:1-11).

The Israelites needed to experience testing in order to check their true acquaintance with God and to check their own hearts. The purpose of the testing and discipline of the wilderness was not to furnish the Israelites with a title to Canaan which they had merited by their own works. Rather, the purpose of these experiences was to acquaint them with God and to reveal to them what their own hearts were like. They had to learn what power was available to them because of their relationship with God. They needed to enlarge their capacity for the enjoyment of Canaan when they actually arrived there.

The purposes of the wilderness experience were specifically mentioned by Moses later when the nation had arrived on the east side of the Jordan River, just before entering the land. Moses told the people, "Thou shalt remember all the way which the Lord thy God led thee these forty years in the wilderness, to humble thee, and to prove thee, to know what was in thine heart, whether thou wouldest keep his commandments, or no. And he humbled thee, and suffered thee to hunger, and fed thee with manna, which thou knewest not, neither did thy fathers know; that he might make thee know that man doth not live by bread only, but by every word that proceedeth out of the mouth of the Lord doth man live" (Deut. 8:2,3).

Travelers and Wanderers

The Israelites might have reasoned that since they were following the cloud, which was an indication of God's presence, they should have an easy road. Many Christians think the same way today. Some believe that if you are in the will of God, you will not experience any difficulty. Therefore, as soon as difficulty comes, they reason that one is not in the will of God. They do not realize, however, that God allows tests in order to mature us in the Christian life (I Pet. 1:6,7).

How sad it is that some who are saved and dedicated to the Lord are completely unprepared to accept the testings that occur through the "wilderness" of life. As believers we must remind ourselves that we are to journey through the wilderness and not just to wander around in it. As long as we are going through the wilderness of this world, we can expect tests along the way, even though we are in the will of God at the time.

Each believer needs to ask himself whether he is a traveler or a wanderer in the Christian life. A traveler goes from one point to another, but a wanderer has no particular goal or sense of direction. He makes his home wherever he is and is unconcerned about progress. Those of us who know Jesus Christ as Saviour need to have a sense of direction as we journey toward heaven. We must not be wanderers, making this world our home and living as if we're going to be here forever.

Faith, or confidence, in God is the determining factor in the way a person lives in this life. If the believer does not think God has great things in mind for him, he will be content to wander in this life without having his eyes fixed on the future. But the believer who has confidence in God will be like Abraham who "looked for a city which hath foundations, whose builder and maker is God" (Heb. 11:10).

Abraham, and the others mentioned in Hebrews 11, lived by faith, as is evident from verse 13: "These all died in faith, not having received the promises, but having seen them afar off, and were persuaded of them, and embraced them, and confessed that they were strangers and pilgrims on the earth." Those of us who know Christ as Saviour should recognize that we, too, are "strangers and pilgrims on the earth."

What a shame that many Christians aimlessly wander in this life with no spiritual purpose at all. In contrast notice the Apostle Paul who had a specific goal in mind. When addressing the Ephesian elders concerning what might happen to him when he went to Jerusalem, Paul said, "But none of these things move me, neither count I my life dear unto myself, so that I might finish my course with joy, and the ministry, which I have received of the Lord Jesus, to testify the gospel of the grace of God" (Acts 20:24). Notice Paul's goal: "That I might finish my course with joy, and the ministry, which I have received of the Lord Jesus."

At the time that Paul spoke these words much of his ministry was still ahead of him. Did he accomplish what he set out to do? The answer is found in the last recorded letter he wrote. Paul wrote: "I am now ready to be offered, and the time of my departure is at hand. I have fought a good fight, I have finished my course, I have kept the faith" (II Tim. 4:6,7).

If you know Jesus Christ as your Saviour, do you have a goal in life? Or are you like a motorboat whose engine is running while the anchor is dropped? Some Christians are anchored to the world and go nowhere spiritually. They may engage in much motion, or activity, but because they are anchored to the world and the desires of the old life, they do not honor Christ in their daily walk.

Those who have trusted Jesus Christ as their personal Saviour have become new creatures and possess new desires (II Cor. 5:17). However, they are not following their new desires if they are going after the things of the world. This in itself is the reason that Christians must be tested—to teach them about themselves as well as the faithfulness of God.

How sad it is to be an unused Christian. It is tests that often change a Christian from uselessness to usefulness. The

Bible reminds us: "Now no chastening for the present seemeth to be joyous, but grievous: nevertheless afterward it yieldeth the peaceable fruit of righteousness unto them which are exercised thereby" (Heb. 12:11).

Purposes of the Wilderness Experience

For Israel, the wilderness experience served two purposes: to teach them about God and His methods and to teach them about themselves.

God had told the Israelites, "I will take you to me for a people, and I will be to you a God: and ye shall know that I am the Lord your God, which bringeth you out from under the burdens of the Egyptians" (Ex. 6:7).

God desires that we today know Him in an intimate way also. We must learn to trust Him in spite of the circumstances and apparent conflicts. The Apostle John wrote: "We know that the Son of God is come, and hath given us an understanding, that we may know him that is true" (I John 5:20). It is important that those who are heaven-bound really know the God of heaven. Do we really know *Him* or do we only know *about* Him?

To some people, heaven is only a beautiful place where the streets are paved with gold. But even that signifies a difference between earthly and heavenly priorities. What is considered most valuable here on earth is used in heaven only as paving on which to walk. The most important part of heaven will be the fact that we will be in the very presence of God and will have fellowship with Him. We must not let the values of this life influence our thinking concerning what will be important in heaven. When we stand in the very presence of God, everything else will be secondary.

God planned for the Israelites to learn to know themselves through the testings they experienced. The testing of the wilderness manifested the evil that was in their hearts, the incurable corruption of the flesh. Although God performed miracle after miracle for them, as soon as they faced the next test, they grumbled and complained as if they had never seen God work in their behalf.

Our testings can also show us what our hearts are really like. We need to be humbled and to prove by experience that entrance into the abundant life is solely a matter of sovereign grace; it is not based on our merits. We need to realize that we are not to have any confidence in our old nature, or flesh, for it can produce nothing good (Rom. 7:18).

The tests we face will be like the wilderness tests of Israel in that they will expose our weaknesses and failures, but they will also magnify the power and longsuffering of God who bought us and then brought us to the place of testing.

To the natural man the world offers much that is attractive and alluring, but to the spiritual man what the world has to offer is only "vanity and vexation of spirit" (Eccles. 1:14). The world offers much to satisfy the lust of the flesh, the lust of the eyes and the pride of life (I John 2:16), but it offers nothing whatever to satisfy the desires of the new nature. Each believer should be able to say with the Apostle Paul, "God forbid that I should glory, save in the cross of our Lord Jesus Christ, by whom the world is crucified unto me, and I unto the world" (Gal. 6:14).

Chapter 10

Bitter Waters

After the Israelites had passed through the Red Sea, "they went out into the wilderness of Shur; and they went three days in the wilderness, and found no water" (Ex. 15:22).

Imagine what a desperate situation it was for all the Israelites to be without water. How glad they must have been when they came to Marah and saw water! But their delight soon ended, because "when they came to Marah, they could not drink of the waters of Marah, for they were bitter" (v. 23).

Even though the Israelites had been miraculously delivered through the Red Sea, they thought now that they were all going to perish for lack of water. The Bible says, "The people murmured against Moses, saying, What shall we drink?" (v. 24). The people thought that the Lord had forgotten all about them and that they would die in the barren wilderness. A short time before they had been praising God for His mighty deliverance; now they had no hope whatsoever that the problem before them could be solved.

You have probably experienced this kind of discouraging situation even as we have. I remember in particular when Mrs. Epp and I had first come to Lincoln, Nebraska, in 1939 to begin the Back to the Bible ministry. We had three small children at the time. About the first week of July our situation was desperate—letters weren't being received, so money wasn't being received either.

I remember walking the floor and trying to find something from the Word of God that would strengthen me and encourage my soul. The only verse which the Lord seemed to keep pounding home to my soul was, "I shall yet praise him" (Ps. 42:5). But I didn't know how I could possibly do that. My attitude was one of murmuring and complaining, and I even expressed to the Lord that I didn't see how I could praise Him for that day. I was really downcast.

My wife, however, recognizing the condition I was in, said, "Well, we can't both be down on the same day." So she went to the Word to find what promise the Lord would give her. She found a promise in Job that she claimed that day: "Though he slay me, yet will I trust in him" (Job 13:15).

All this took place on July 5. A month later we received a letter from a missionary friend in Africa. Enclosed was an American $5 bill. There was only a brief note saying, "God laid it on my heart to send you this money for the radio." When I looked at the date on the letter, I noticed that it had been written on July 5! I praised the Lord that day because it settled an important issue in my life. It proved that God would take care of those who committed their way to Him.

Murmuring and Complaining

The Israelites felt sorry for themselves in the desert, for even though they had water, it was so bitter they couldn't drink it. However, the clue to what God was doing through this test is found in the last words of Exodus 15:25: "There he proved them." This first test which the Israelites experienced after they had passed through the Red Sea was designed to teach them (and through them to teach us) that nothing the world had to offer would satisfy their most basic needs. The Israelites had to learn to trust God to supply their needs, and we have to learn the same lesson.

The believer needs to realize that the waters of this world are bitter and totally unsatisfactory when it comes to meeting his most basic spiritual needs. In His discussion with the woman at the well, Jesus kept emphasizing that those who drink of the waters of this world will thirst again but that those who drink of the water He has to offer will never thirst again (John 4:13,14). Jesus invited all to drink of the water He has to offer: "If any man thirst, let him come unto me, and drink" (7:37).

Many believers do not realize that they will experience tests and trials in their lives after redemption. God does not want us to settle down and be content in this world; in fact, Jesus made it clear that in this world there would be severe problems. He said, "Peace I leave with you, my peace I give unto you: not as the world giveth, give I unto you. Let not your heart be troubled, neither let it be afraid" (14:27). Jesus told believers, "If the world hate you, ye know that it hated me before it hated you. If ye were of the world, the world would love his own: but because ye are not of the world, but I have chosen you out of the world, therefore the world hateth you" (15:18,19). He also said, "In the world ye shall have tribulation: but be of good cheer; I have overcome the world" (16:33).

So we see that only God has something to offer us that really satisfies. And He wants to teach us through the tests we face to depend only on Him to fully meet our needs. He wants to teach us His ways and His values. We need to learn to trust God not only when times are good but also when there seems to be no solution to the problem. We need to realize that even though we do not know how God is going to solve the problem, "all things work together for good to them that love God, to them who are the called according to his purpose" (Rom. 8:28). This means that we must recognize His sovereignty and ability to accomplish what He knows is best both for us and for Him.

Even the Apostle Paul had to learn these lessons in his own life. Yet, he was eventually able to say, "Not that I speak in respect of want: for I have learned, in whatsoever state I am, therewith to be content. I know both how to be abased, and I know how to abound: every where and in all things I am instructed both to be full and to be hungry, both to abound and to suffer need. I can do all things through Christ which strengtheneth me" (Phil. 4:11-13).

Only three days after the Red Sea experience the Israelites were grumbling against Moses and against God. Three days before they had been singing, now they were complaining. The people had said, "The Lord is my strength and song, and he is become my salvation: he is my God, and I will prepare him an habitation; my father's God, and I will exalt him. . . . Who is like unto thee, O Lord, among the gods? Who is like thee, glorious in holiness, fearful in praises, doing wonders? . . . Thou in thy mercy hast led forth the people which thou hast redeemed: thou hast guided them in thy strength unto thy holy habitation" (Ex. 15:2,11,13).

What went wrong? Why such a change of attitude in just three days? They had overlooked the fact that the cloud had led them in this direction, and since God was leading them, He would supply their needs.

When the people murmured against Moses (v. 24), they were actually murmuring against God, because Moses was God's representative to lead them. Every complaint against circumstances, every grumbling about the daily trials of life is directed against the One who "worketh all things after the counsel of his own will" (Eph. 1:11). Although the Israelites did not have this verse at the time, they had seen enough of God's work to know that He did not make mistakes and that He could perform anything necessary to provide for them. And remember, what happened to Israel is to serve as an example to us (I Cor. 10:11).

Notice what Moses' reaction was when the people murmured against him: "He cried unto the Lord" (Ex. 15:25). While the people were blaming him for their situation, Moses was calling out to the Lord. What a great example this is for us, demonstrating that we should turn everything over to God.

Concerning this matter I have especially appreciated Psalm 37:5: "Commit thy way unto the Lord; trust also in him; and he shall bring it to pass." Notice also I Peter 5:7: "Casting all your care upon him; for he careth for you." Psalm 55:22 conveys the same thought: "Cast thy burden upon the Lord, and he shall sustain thee: he shall never suffer the righteous to be moved."

How important it is that we keep "looking unto Jesus the author and finisher of our faith" (Heb. 12:2). Our confidence must be in Him, not in ourselves.

The Tree

As Moses called out to God in his need, God revealed what Moses should do. "The Lord shewed him a tree, which when he had cast into the waters, the waters were made sweet" (Ex. 15:25). This place was called Marah, meaning "bitter," but now it had become "sweet." Our Marahs, or testings, are for the purpose of driving us to Jesus Christ, even as God used this Marah to prove the Israelites (v. 25). Even though the bitter waters were a bad experience at first, it was used to draw the people closer to the Lord. So also, even though chastening is difficult for us to bear, the results are good (Heb. 12:11).

Romans 5 shows the method by which God works in the lives of believers: "We glory in tribulations also: knowing that tribulation worketh patience; and patience, experience; and experience, hope: and hope maketh not ashamed; because the love of God is shed abroad in our hearts by the Holy Ghost which is given unto us" (vv. 3-5).

How can anyone glory in tribulation? The answer is given in Romans 5:1,2: "Therefore being justified by faith, we have peace with God through our Lord Jesus Christ: by whom also we have access by faith into this grace wherein we stand, and rejoice in hope of the glory of God." When we recognize that our position is secure in Christ, we will be willing to endure tribulation. We can then realize that it will give us a greater understanding of who God is and of the way He wants to work in our lives.

Notice that God instructed Moses to throw a tree into the bitter waters to make them sweet (Ex. 15:25). This tree is a reminder of the cross of the Lord Jesus Christ. All that we have is related to what Christ accomplished for us. He suffered, He died on the cross (tree), He was buried, He rose from the dead and He ascended to the Father. The Bible says, "Who his own self bare our sins in his own body on the tree, that we, being dead to sins, should live unto righteousness: by whose stripes ye were healed" (I Pet. 2:24). We are also told, "Christ hath redeemed us from the curse of the law, being made a curse for us: for it is written, Cursed is every one that hangeth on a tree" (Gal. 3:13).

So the tree that Moses threw into the bitter waters to make them sweet points us to all that Jesus Christ accomplished for us in relation to the cross. There He accomplished a work for us, but now He is working in us. No wonder Paul said, "God forbid that I should glory, save in the cross of our Lord Jesus Christ" (6:14).

Suffering for God

As those of us who know Christ glory in the cross and all that is related to it, we will realize that our lives will involve suffering. In fact, suffering weans us from dependence on the world.

Paul desired to really know God, and he realized that this involved suffering: "That I may know him, and the power of his resurrection, and the fellowship of his sufferings, being made conformable unto his death" (Phil. 3:10).

Paul recognized that any suffering the believer endured in this life could not be compared with the rewards to come. He said, "If children, then heirs; heirs of God, and joint-heirs with Christ; if so be that we suffer with him, that we may be also glorified together. For I reckon that the sufferings of this present time are not worthy to be compared with the glory which shall be revealed in us" (Rom. 8:17,18).

Paul had much to say about suffering. To Timothy he wrote: "Therefore I endure all things for the elect's sakes, that they may also obtain the salvation which is in Christ Jesus with eternal glory. It is a faithful saying: For if we be dead with him, we shall also live with him: if we suffer, we shall also reign with him: if we deny him, he also will deny us" (II Tim. 2:10-12). The denying that Paul referred to was not denying Jesus Christ as Saviour but denying His way, His methods and His purpose. If we refuse to accept these matters, God will deny us rewards that would result from suffering for Him.

If those who know Christ as Saviour murmur and complain against man and God as the Israelites did, the result will be a spiritually stunted life. They will only prove their immaturity.

God always works in our lives to bring about spiritual growth and maturity. It is not enough to know information; one must act upon it. God revealed to Moses that a nearby tree should be thrown into the bitter waters, but the waters would have remained bitter had Moses not acted on God's instructions. Notice that Moses did not provide the cure, he only applied it. This reminds us again of Romans 6. God has provided the cure for the sin problem both before and after we become His children, but we must apply it by faith in order to benefit from it. Victory comes in Christian living only as we take God at His Word and live accordingly. Of course, the basis for all of our victory is that we have been "justified by faith" (Rom. 5:1).

A Place of Refreshing

After the incident at Marah, the Israelites "came to Elim, where were twelve wells of water, and threescore and ten palm trees: and they encamped there by the waters" (Ex. 15:27).

From this verse we see the principle that blessing follows testing. The Israelites were tested at Marah, where God revealed His power to take care of every need they had. Then they found an abundance of water and shelter at Elim. Whereas Marah was a place of testing, Elim was a place of refreshing. Elim was a foretaste of what they would have once they entered Canaan. This foretaste was like earnest money given as an indication that the purchaser will follow through on his promise. The New Testament reveals that the Holy Spirit is the earnest for the believer—the indication that God will follow through on all He has promised (Eph. 1:13,14).

The Israelites had no unfulfilled needs or wants at Elim. They could have said as did David, "The Lord is my shepherd; I shall not want. He maketh me to lie down in green pastures: he leadeth me beside the still waters. He restoreth my soul: he leadeth me in the paths of righteousness for his name's sake" (Ps. 23:1-3).

Notice that David said, "He maketh me to lie down in green pastures." We might not always want to go where the Lord wants us to, but through the testing which He allows, He makes us come to the place of refreshing.

The person who relies on God for his daily needs and rejoices in the person of God is truly blessed. David told of the person who is blessed by God: "Blessed is the man that walketh not in the counsel of the ungodly, nor standeth in the way of sinners, nor sitteth in the seat of the scornful. But his delight is in the law of the Lord; and in his law doth he meditate day and night. And he shall be like a tree planted by the rivers of water, that bringeth forth his fruit in his season;

his leaf also shall not wither; and whatsoever he doeth shall prosper" (1:1-3). When we realize how good the Lord is to those who love Him and walk in His way, we can say with the psalmist, "O magnify the Lord with me, and let us exalt his name together" (34:3).

At this stage in Israel's history, God was just beginning His work to bring them to full strength—to bring them to the point of spiritual maturity that He desired. God also works in believers today to bring about that which pleases Him. In fact, God has given gifted men to the Church whose purpose it is to equip the saints to do the work of the ministry: "He gave some, apostles; and some, prophets; and some, evangelists; and some, pastors and teachers; for the perfecting [equipping] of the saints, for the work of the ministry, for the edifying of the body of Christ: till we all come in the unity of the faith, and of the knowledge of the Son of God, unto a perfect [mature] man, unto the measure of the stature of the fulness of Christ" (Eph. 4:11-13). Again, we can be assured that whatever process God begins, He will complete (Phil. 1:6).

Chapter 11

Manna From Heaven

After experiencing the blessing of the 12 wells of water and the 70 palm trees, the Israelites "took their journey from Elim, and all the congregation of the children of Israel came unto the wilderness of Sin, which is between Elim and Sinai, on the fifteenth day of the second month after their departing out of the land of Egypt" (Ex. 16:1).

Moses' Great Faith

The Israelites were on their way toward Mt. Sinai where the Law would be given by God through Moses. Moses demonstrated great faith and courage as he led the Israelites in this direction, which took them through the barren desert, farther and farther from the supplies of the outside world. For the first time, the real emptiness and privation of the desert probably stared Moses and his people in the face. Until then they had been near populated areas, but they were leaving civilization for the barren, wind-swept desert. Their journey took them farther and farther from any population center, and humanly speaking, they seemed headed for certain death.

Imagine—about three million people were led by Moses into the howling waste of the desert! Remember, Moses was not ignorant of conditions in the desert—he had spent time there being prepared by God for the very task he was now performing. But no matter what kind of leadership genius Moses had, it would take constant provision by miracles of God to sustain the Israelites in the desert. And Moses knew

93

this because he had spent 40 years there learning spiritual lessons he would never forget.

Some believers go into situations that they do not know about, and they must rely on God to lead them. But Moses' faith was even greater because he knew the obstacles and went anyhow. This reminds us of Abraham, of whom the Bible says, "By faith Abraham, when he was called to go out into a place which he should after receive for an inheritance, obeyed; and he went out, not knowing whither he went" (Heb. 11:8). Yet when famine came, Abraham went down to Egypt (Gen. 12:10).

Moses knew his obstacles ahead of time and demonstrated unreserved faith in God. His experiences with Pharaoh and of seeing God work now paid off.

Moses' Leadership Tested

Believers today must be spiritually strong in Christ so they can face tests. The Bible instructs believers how they ought to live: "As ye have therefore received Christ Jesus the Lord, so walk ye in him: rooted and built up in him, and stablished in the faith, as ye have been taught, abounding therein with thanksgiving" (Col. 2:6,7). A person is saved by faith and is to live by faith. Only then is the believer able to face the tests that God allows to come into his life.

The Apostle Paul had undergone many severe tests, but his testimony was: "Thanks be to God, which giveth us the victory through our Lord Jesus Christ" (I Cor. 15:57). Because of the victory that is always possible in Christ, Paul went on to urge believers, "Therefore, my beloved brethren, be ye stedfast, unmoveable, always abounding in the work of the Lord, forasmuch as ye know that your labour is not in vain in the Lord" (v. 58).

The test that Moses was about to undergo had to do with his leadership. The Israelites grumbled against him and said, "Would to God we had died by the hand of the Lord in the land of Egypt, when we sat by the flesh pots, and when we did eat bread to the full; for ye have brought us forth into this wilderness, to kill this whole assembly with hunger" (Ex. 16:3). The Bible reveals, however, that the murmurings of the Israelites were really directed against the Lord (v. 7).

Only a month had elapsed since the Israelites had left Egypt, and they were already questioning God's goodness and greatness. This reveals the total depravity of man. God had delivered them from Egypt by miracle after miracle, yet they grumbled and complained when they encountered a problem. And it wasn't that there were just a few people who grumbled—"the whole congregation of the children of Israel murmured" (v. 2). What a sad situation. How this must have grieved Moses, and how it especially must have grieved the heart of God!

The psalmist, in commenting on this incident, said, "They sinned yet more against him by provoking the most High in the wilderness. And they tempted God in their heart by asking meat for their lust. Yea, they spake against God; they said, Can God furnish a table in the wilderness?" (Ps. 78:17-19). So the divine commentary on the incident in Exodus is that the people, though they grumbled against Moses, were actually speaking against God. They questioned God's ability to take care of them.

The sin of the Israelites was even worse in that they took an oath, as indicated by the expression "Would to God we had died" (Ex. 16:3). This amounted to taking the name of the Lord in vain.

In their rebellion and unbelief the Israelites lied about their former situation. They said that in Egypt they "sat by the flesh pots" and ate "bread to the full" (v. 3). How a little bit of time had affected their memories!

The Israelites had forgotten that they were actually slaves in Egypt. Their gathering of gold, silver and jewelry before they left Egypt was a matter of picking up their back wages. Their situation as slaves had not been good at all, but they had forgotten this.

What about their song of victory, recorded in Exodus 15? At that time they were so thankful to the Lord, but a month later they had forgotten their hard taskmasters in Egypt and the goodness of the Lord in delivering them from Egypt. At the Red Sea they had realized that God was not only leading them out of Egypt but that He was also leading them into the land (v. 13).

What the Israelites needed to do at this time was to count their blessings. Since God had delivered them many times before, would He now forsake them? They should have known God better than that. But murmurers and complainers are shortsighted. The cloud had not left them; they were still under it. It not only provided them with the guidance of God but also gave them shade from the hot sun. But they thought God had completely forsaken them. They were right where God wanted them, and they should have realized that even though they did not understand what God was doing, it was for their best.

How fickle people can be. The Israelites were singing songs of praises on one day and complaining to God on the next. Remember, when we murmur at the circumstances God brings into our lives, we are actually murmuring against Him.

Moses' Reactions

Moses did not try to defend himself; he simply went to the Lord and then faithfully delivered to the people the instructions he received from the Lord. What an interesting study it is to observe the reactions of Moses at times like this. He loved his people dearly and was giving his life to lead them from Egypt to Canaan, yet they frequently complained against him. But their murmurings only drew him closer to the Lord. How about us? When others complain against us, are we driven to the Lord for counsel and direction? Because Moses had seen God work so mightily in the past, he was willing to trust God now without question.

Let us not be like the Israelites who complained against the Lord. We often tend to feel sorry for ourselves and to question God's goodness, but we should instead remind ourselves of all that He has done for us. Jesus Christ has paid the penalty for our sins so we can be delivered from eternal condemnation, and He has provided all we need to live a life of victory. So in times of discouragement, let us stop and count our blessings before we question the goodness of God.

The reactions of Moses proved what a gentle and great man he really was. No wonder the Bible says, "(Now the man Moses was very meek, above all the men which were upon the face of the earth)" (Num. 12:3).

As the people grumbled against Moses, God took up his case and fought in his behalf. Having trusted in Jesus Christ as Saviour, we can rely on Him to take care of any situation. Paul expressed it in these words: "I know whom I have believed, and am persuaded that he is able to keep that which I have committed unto him against that day" (II Tim. 1:12). Is this the kind of confidence you have in God? Each believer can have the assurance that God will work to defend the believer who seeks to glorify Him.

Consider what trials accomplish in our lives. Before Job had experienced severe testing, he did not have nearly as great a concept of God as he did later. After experiencing his trials, Job said, "I have heard of thee by the hearing of the ear: but now mine eye seeth thee. Wherefore I abhor myself, and repent in dust and ashes" (Job 42:5,6). Think of some of the other statements Job made: "He knoweth the way that I take: when he hath tried me, I shall come forth as gold" (23:10); "Though he slay me, yet will I trust in him" (13:15).

Consider what a test David went through when he and the men under his leadership discovered that their wives and children had been taken captive. David was blamed for negligence in letting them be captured; in fact, the men were even considering stoning David to death. But the Bible says, "David encouraged himself in the Lord his God" (I Sam. 30:6). No matter what the test, that's what the Lord wants each of us to do—to encourage ourselves in Him.

Notice the reaction of the psalmist when he was tested: "Be merciful unto me, O God: for man would swallow me up; he fighting daily oppresseth me. Mine enemies would daily swallow me up: for they be many that fight against me, O thou most High. What time I am afraid, I will trust in thee. In God I will praise his word, in God I have put my trust; I will not fear what flesh can do unto me. Every day they wrest my words: all their thoughts are against me for evil" (Ps. 56:1-5).

Perhaps you think that you would never murmur against God as the Israelites did, but think of some of the statements you may have made or thoughts you may have had under adverse circumstances. I've heard believers say, "Why did God take my husband?" or "Why did God take my wife?" or "Why did God take my child?" While such questions can be asked simply as a result of the frustration of the moment, some ask such questions in bitterness of soul, actually questioning God's wisdom and goodness.

Bread from Heaven

But how good God is, even to those who blame Him for difficult circumstances! When the Israelites grumbled against God, He told Moses, "Behold, I will rain bread from heaven for you; and the people shall go out and gather a certain rate every day, that I may prove them, whether they will walk in my law, or no" (Ex. 16:4).

Surely this was amazing grace—that God would perform a miracle to bring bread from heaven to feed complainers! It's more logical to think that He would rain fire from heaven to destroy them rather than bread from heaven to feed them. How wonderfully great and amazing is the mercy of the Lord! "Who is a God like unto thee, that pardoneth iniquity, and passeth by the transgression of the remnant of his heritage? He retaineth not his anger for ever, because he delighteth in mercy" (Mic. 7:18).

A word that stands out in the psalms of David is "mercy." David delighted in the mercy of God because he knew what it was to experience God's grace and forgiveness.

Comparing the nation of Israel to an individual, Israel was a new man with a heavenly nature and had need of heavenly food. Ephesians 1:3 tells us, "Blessed be the God and Father of our Lord Jesus Christ, who hath blessed us with all spiritual blessings in heavenly places in Christ." God has made available all the heavenly food that we will ever need.

In Israel's case food actually descended from heaven for them to gather. In commenting on this incident later, the psalmist referred to the manna as "angels' food" (Ps. 78:25).

Manna is a beautiful type of the food which God provides for our souls. The Word of God—both the living, incarnate Word and the written Word—provides food for our souls. Of course, even the written Word is living, as indicated in Hebrews 4:12: "For the word of God is quick [living], and powerful, and sharper than any twoedged sword, piercing even to the dividing asunder of soul and spirit, and of the joints and marrow, and is a discerner of the thoughts and intents of the heart."

The flesh pots that the Israelites remembered in Egypt belonged to earth, but manna belonged to heaven. Sometimes the Israelites were faced with the question of which they enjoyed most, the food of earth or the food of heaven. It is good for each believer to reflect on what he enjoys most—the things of the world or the things of heaven.

Remember, the provision of the manna was for the purpose of proving, or testing, Israel (Ex. 16:4). The Israelites had been delivered physically from Egypt, but God was concerned about their heart, or desires, being delivered from Egypt also. Later, not everyone appreciated the manna God sent from heaven (Num. 11:4-6). Though they appreciated it at first because it kept them from starvation, they grew weary of this miraculous provision from heaven.

Just as the extent of enjoyment the Israelites had in the manna determined whether the desires of their hearts were fixed on God or Egypt, so the believer's attitude toward God reveals whether his attention is fixed on Christ or on the things of the world. Each believer needs to ask himself, Does Christ truly satisfy me? Am I taken up with Him? Do I have to have other things in addition to Christ to be satisfied?

When referring to Himself as the Bread of Life, Jesus compared Himself and His Word to the manna that came down from heaven (John 6:22-59). Jesus is the Word, and He said, "I am the living bread which came down from heaven: if any man eat of this bread, he shall live for ever: and the bread that I will give is my flesh, which I will give for the life of the world" (v. 51).

Christ is the living Word, but He is revealed to us in the written Word. We know of Him and we assimilate truths about Him as we study the written Word. The written Word tells of the living Word who was made flesh and dwelt among men (1:14). So we need to feed on the written Word because it reveals to us the incarnate, living Word, Jesus Christ Himself.

So the manna of the Old Testament prefigured Jesus Christ as revealed in the New Testament. This is why Jesus explained, "Moses gave you not that bread from heaven; but my Father giveth you the true bread from heaven. For the bread of God is he which cometh down from heaven, and giveth life unto the world" (6:32,33). When His listeners

asked for His bread, Jesus said, "I am the bread of life: he
that cometh to me shall never hunger; and he that believeth
on me shall never thirst" (v. 35). Let us feed on the written
Word of God in order that we may feed on the living Word.

Two Natures

The person who knows Jesus Christ as Saviour has two
natures. He has the old nature, or Adamic nature, which he
had when he was born into this life. This nature is referred to
in the Bible as the flesh. This nature enjoys the things of the
world and is particularly concerned about fitting into the
world system and all that it has to offer. But the believer also
has a new nature, which he received when he trusted Jesus
Christ as personal Saviour. This new nature is satisfied only
with heavenly food. The worldly Christian is one who,
although a believer, desires the things of the world system.
Worldliness is more an attitude toward the world than a
particular behavior pattern.

Because the believer has two natures, he must decide to
which nature he will yield. Both natures are vying for his
attention, but he can yield to only one at a time, so he must
make a choice. Paul told believers, "Neither yield ye your
members as instruments of unrighteousness unto sin: but
yield yourselves unto God, as those that are alive from the
dead, and your members as instruments of righteousness unto
God" (Rom. 6:13). He asked, "Know ye not, that to whom
ye yield yourselves servants to obey, his servants ye are to
whom ye obey; whether of sin unto death, or of obedience
unto righteousness?" (v. 16). Perhaps some wonder how they
are to yield themselves to God and to righteousness. Paul
explained, "I speak after the manner of men because of the
infirmity of your flesh: for as ye have yielded your members
servants to uncleanness and to iniquity unto iniquity; even so
now yield your members servants to righteousness unto
holiness" (v. 19).

God promised to take care of the spiritual needs of the
Israelites. He was going to "rain bread from heaven" for them
(Ex. 16:4). Notice it was bread "from heaven." Its origin was
not in this world, even as the bread which the believer today
is to feed on is not of this world. The living Word, Jesus

Christ, is God, so He is eternal. Although He entered this world by being born of flesh, He did not have His origin in this world. Neither is the origin of the written Word in this world. Second Timothy 3:16 reveals its origin: "All scripture is given by inspiration of God [is God-breathed]." Although God uses human authors to write the Scriptures, He is the One who superintended so that they chose precisely the words He wanted them to choose. So as we study the written Word in order to feed on the living Word, we are actually gaining spiritual strength from that which originates outside the world.

Referring to the manna, Moses told the Israelites, "In the morning, then ye shall see the glory of the Lord" (Ex. 16:7). The manna was a type of Jesus Christ, who referred to Himself as "the bread of life" (John 6:35). To grow spiritually, a believer must feed on Jesus Christ, who is the living Word, and He is revealed only in the written Word, the Bible. It is impossible to know more about Christ unless one knows more about the Bible.

The Israelites gathered manna in the morning and had the glory of the Lord revealed to them, just as a believer will see the glory of the Lord as he reads and meditates on the Word of God each day. Although it is not essential to have a devotional time in the morning, many Christians find that this is the best part of the day for this special time with the Lord. What a difference it will make in our lives as we daily read and meditate on God's Word and see His glory revealed to us!

Think of the abundant provision God made for the Israelites in the manna. The Israelites were to gather "an omer for every man" (Ex. 16:16). An omer equaled about six pints. Assuming there were about 3 million people, this would mean that they gathered more than 18 million pints of manna a day. Think of this tremendous quantity! And God provided this not only for one day or for several days but for 40 years. They thought they would starve in the desert, but God took care of them abundantly.

Gathering and Using the Manna

Notice that the manna was found wherever the cloud was located. As long as the Israelites stayed where God wanted them to be, their needs were taken care of. Any individual who left the accompanying cloud and traveled on his own would not have his needs taken care of. But wherever the cloud, which was the indication of God's presence with the people, was found, there was sustenance.

Notice also that the Israelites did not have to go a long distance to get groceries. The manna fell near them. So also, the Word is constantly available to us. Not only is the living Word everywhere present, but we also have the written Word available on every hand. Most homes in North America have more than one copy or translation of the Bible, so the written Word is easily accessible to all. The Israelites either had to gather the manna or trample it underfoot. What a parallel this is to us concerning the Word of God! We either read and obey it, or we trample its truths underfoot. What are you doing with the Word of God?

The manna came in the form of "a small round thing" (Ex. 16:14). So also, the written Word is not a big library—all 66 books are contained in a relatively small volume. Yet more truth is contained in this one small volume than in the greatest of libraries. In this one small volume God has revealed all we need to know in order to bring us into right relationship with Himself and to enable us to live a life of victory.

The Bible reveals that the manna the Israelites were provided with was white (v. 31). This color is the symbol of purity, and certainly the Word of God is pure. The psalmist said, "The words of the Lord are pure words: as silver tried in a furnace of earth, purified seven times" (Ps. 12:6). Also the purity of the Word is seen in the words "holy scriptures" (II Tim. 3:15). There is no mixture of falsehood, or error, with truth. The original writings contained no mistakes, no contradictions, no blemishes. What a wonderful revelation God has given us!

God gave the Israelites manna to eat. It did them no good if they only looked at it or considered it something to be admired. So also, the written Word of God has been given to us for more than intellectual admiration; it is spiritual food to us as we assimilate its truths. It is one thing to know information from or about the Word of God on an intellectual level, but it's quite another thing to apply those truths to one's life. Only when it is applied does the person come into right relationship with Jesus Christ and grow to spiritual maturity.

Although we should study the Bible for the doctrine it contains, we should look beyond the doctrine to see the person it reveals, the Lord Jesus Christ. We must see Christ as more than a mere historical person. We must see Him as the Scriptures reveal Him—as God, as Redeemer and as life itself.

The Bible itself has much to say about the Word of God. Sometime try using Psalm 119 during your devotional time and consider the various ways that the Word of God is referred to in this psalm. The entire psalm has 176 verses which are divided into segments of eight verses each. When originally written in Hebrew, the first eight verses began with the first letter of the Hebrew alphabet, the second eight verses began with the second letter of the alphabet, and so on. In your devotional time consider eight verses each day. As you meditate on the verses, you will see the many references to the Word of God and will realize more than ever how important it is to the believer's life.

When we study the Scriptures, we recognize that Jesus Christ is far more than just a person who lived long ago; He is more than the "historical Jesus." In reality Jesus Christ is eternal life itself. The Bible says, "This is the record, that God hath given to us eternal life, and this life is in his Son. He that hath the Son hath life; and he that hath not the Son of God hath not life" (I John 5:11,12). Since Jesus Christ is life, we not only receive eternal life by trusting Him as personal Saviour, but we gain spiritual strength as we feed on the written Word which reveals Him to us.

In regard to spiritual food, three words sum up what a believer needs to do: appropriate, masticate and assimilate.

Appropriating

It is obvious that the Israelites had to gather the manna as it came from heaven. God did not force it down their throats; rather, the Israelites had to take the responsibility of gathering it. Benefiting from the manna involved a condition; it had to be gathered.

Both the provision and condition concerning salvation are seen in John 3:16. The provision is, "For God so loved the world, that he gave his only begotten Son." The condition involved is seen in the words, "that whosoever believeth in him should not perish, but have everlasting life." As the Israelites had to gather the manna, so a person has to receive Christ as Saviour. "As many as received him, to them gave he power to become the sons of God, even to them that believe on his name" (1:12).

Joshua 1:3 also reveals both God's part and Israel's part in claiming the Promised Land: "Every place that the sole of your foot shall tread upon, that have I given unto you, as I said unto Moses." God had given the land to the Israelites, but they had to go in and actually take it.

To appropriate the Word of God is to take it to ourselves; it is to make it our own. We come to the Word of God with all of our needs, and then we apply what the Bible says to our needs. When we believe God and obey His Word, we are appropriating it. The believer feeds on Christ as he lives by His promises (Col. 2:6,7).

Masticating

Having appropriated spiritual food, we then need to masticate it. That is, we need to meditate on it; we must determine to make it our own. This involves more than just a quick reading of the Word or even taking time in the Word; it involves reflecting on the truths we see in the Word and applying them to our personal needs.

The psalmist had much to say about meditating on God's Word. Concerning the man who is blessed, the psalmist said, "His delight is in the law of the Lord; and in his law doth he meditate day and night. And he shall be like a tree planted by the rivers of water, that bringeth forth his fruit in his season; his leaf also shall not wither; and whatsoever he doeth shall prosper" (Ps. 1:2,3).

Notice the following statements in Psalm 119: "Open thou mine eyes, that I may behold wondrous things out of thy law" (v. 18); "How sweet are thy words unto my taste! Yea, sweeter than honey to my mouth!" (v. 103); "The entrance of thy words giveth light; it giveth understanding unto the simple" (v. 130).

It is regrettable that today the art of meditation on God's Word seems to have been lost. Believers are too busy; they are involved in too many other things. But it is tremendously important that we spend time in God's Word and meditate on its truths. Satan will do everything he can to keep the believer from having time for God's Word. He realizes that time spent meditating on the truths of God's Word is the believer's secret to spiritual power. If Satan cannot keep a person from Christ, he will endeavor to keep him immature by discouraging him from studying and meditating on God's Word, the basis for spiritual growth.

One way to have the Word of God readily available for meditation is to memorize it. The psalmist said, "Thy word have I hid in mine heart, that I might not sin against thee" (v. 11). You may memorize God's Word by the verse or by the chapter; but memorize it. You will discover progress in your spiritual life as you have it available at all times for meditation.

Another way to meditate on God's Word is to write out the verses you are studying. Perhaps you will want to combine writing down verses with memorizing them. You can write them on cards, which will help to fix the verses in your mind, and then you can carry the cards with you to memorize, review and meditate on when you find available time. I often meditate on verses during my morning walk. Sometimes I don't get past one verse for a whole mile because I find so much in it, and God uses it to speak to my heart. At other times I'll review and meditate on several verses during this same time. But the important thing is that we meditate, whatever our method.

Assimilating

In addition to appropriating and masticating the Word of God, we also need to assimilate it. We do this as we comprehend the Word. This takes time, just as it takes time for physical food to be assimilated and to strengthen the body. This is the whole purpose of appropriating and masticating— that one may have spiritual strength and growth.

Jeremiah referred to this whole process when he said, "Thy words were found, and I did eat them; and thy word was unto me the joy and rejoicing of mine heart" (Jer. 15:16). Assimilating the Word of God is not only the means of spiritual nourishment, but it is also a safeguard against temptation and error. This is why the psalmist said, "Thy word have I hid in mine heart, that I might not sin against thee" (Ps. 119:11).

We need to assimilate God's Word not only for salvation but also for our daily walk. Christ saves us from condemnation, but He does much more than that; He also sustains us spiritually. To know Christ for salvation and to grow in Him are two distinct matters, although both are accomplished by faith (Col. 2:6,7).

What are you feeding on today? Is it God's Word or is it television programs or books that dishonor Him? Of course, even activities that do not dishonor Him may rob you of time that you should be spending in His Word. Each of us needs to be very careful in our use of time.

Notice that the Israelites were to gather the manna every day (see Ex. 16:4). What they gathered on one day would not keep until the next. They could not hoard enough or store enough to last a week or a month. If they tried to store it, it would breed worms (vv. 19,20).

Moses instructed the Israelites, "Let no man leave of it till the morning" (v. 19). However, there are always those who refuse to follow instructions, and this was the case concerning the Israelites. But notice what happened to the manna they stored up: "It bred worms, and stank" (v. 20).

It was necessary for the Israelites to gather the manna every morning, for it came with the dew of the morning and melted when the sun became hot (vv. 14,21).

This should be a lesson to us—we must use the Word of God as we gather it. Some Christians seem to want only to take in information about the Word of God without applying it to their lives. But this is not using the Word as it is gathered. Such people may become intellectual giants, but they lack the spiritual insight that God wants them to have and which they attain as they apply the Word to daily life situations.

The Lord Jesus Christ had to tell the Church of Ephesus: "Nevertheless I have somewhat against thee, because thou hast left thy first love. Remember therefore from whence thou art fallen, and repent, and do the first works; or else I will come unto thee quickly, and will remove thy candlestick out of his place, except thou repent" (Rev. 2:4,5). This local church had left its first love. They didn't lose it; they left it. It is an accident when we lose something, but it is either by intent or neglect that we leave something. Many Christians, through neglect, have left their first love because they have not studied the Word of God as they should have. As a result, God takes the testimony away from the believer.

Just as we should not expect one meal to last us all week, neither should we expect time and meditation spent in the Word of God on Monday to last us for several days. We are not to rely on the past but are to daily appropriate, masticate and assimilate the Word of God.

Manna in the Morning

Notice especially that there was a precise time when the Israelites were to gather the manna. The Bible says, "When the dew that lay was gone up, behold, upon the face of the wilderness there lay a small round thing, as small as the hoar frost on the ground" (Ex. 16:14). This verse reveals that the manna came early in the morning.

Did they have all day to gather the manna? The answer is found in verse 21, which says, "When the sun waxed hot, it melted." Both of these verses imply that the manna was to be gathered in the morning.

So also, it is important that the believer's daily devotional period be early in the morning before his mind becomes cluttered with the things of the day.

The usual objection to having the devotional period in the morning is lack of time. It is true that you probably do not have enough time to do a lengthy study in God's Word, such as reading several chapters or a book of the Bible, in the morning. However, remember that the quality of the devotional period is more important than the quantity. Even if you don't have much time, if you determine to do so, you can find sufficient time to read and meditate on a chapter, or at least several verses, in order to get some truth that you can take with you throughout the day. Having seen some truth that you can especially apply to your life, you can then spend time in prayer, asking God to make the truth a reality in your life. Pray also for His guidance and spiritual strength throughout the day. Longer periods of study can be reserved for later in the day.

Just as the manna was fresh in the morning, so we find that the Word of God is fresh for us in the morning and speaks to our hearts in a way that is often not possible later in the day when we are mentally tired or our minds are cluttered with other things. It is not good to read God's Word just to fulfill a requirement; read His Word with a hungry heart to learn more about Him and what you can do to please Him.

In my devotional time I read a chapter, or perhaps two or three chapters. But the important thing is that I read until God draws my attention to a truth or to a verse that I especially need. Sometimes I then write the verse on a card so that I may later memorize it or at least have it available to read and meditate on during the day.

It is important that those of us who know Jesus Christ as Saviour have Him in first place in our lives. If our priorities are not in the right order, we will not be in His Word as we ought to be and our hearts will grow colder. Our lives will become feeble and barren. Remember, the written Word reveals to us the living Word.

The only way to have time for a devotional period is to determine that you will make time for it in your schedule. Just as we set aside time to eat and to do other things, we need to set aside time for the most important matter—fellowship with God.

Concerning the importance of meeting God in the morning in a devotional period, the following poem entitled "The Secret" has been of much encouragement to me:

> I met God in the morning,
> When my day was at its best;
> And His presence came like sunrise
> With a glory in my breast.

All day long His presence lingered,
All day long He stayed with me;
And we sailed in perfect calmness
O'er a very troubled sea.

Other ships were blown and battered,
Other ships were sore distressed,
But the winds that seemed to drive them,
Brought to us, both peace and rest.

Then I thought of other mornings,
With a keen remorse of mind,
When I, too, had loosed the moorings,
With the Presence left behind.

So I think I know the secret,
Learned from many a troubled way;
You must seek Him in the morning,
If you want Him through the day.

—Ralph Cushman

Our Attitudes in Devotions

The Scriptures indicate that the manna fell on the ground (Ex. 16:14). It is doubtful that there were any trees or even bushes for it to fall on, so the Israelites had to stoop to gather it. Even this is a reminder of how we worship the Lord in our devotional time. Either we actually kneel as we pray, or at least we bow in reverence before Almighty God. What a beautiful picture of how we worship God and glean spiritual food from the Bible. We are to depend totally on the Holy Spirit to take the things of God and to make them real to us.

Jesus told His disciples concerning the Holy Spirit, "I have yet many things to say unto you, but ye cannot bear them now. Howbeit when he, the Spirit of truth, is come, he will guide you into all truth: for he shall not speak of himself; but whatsoever he shall hear, that shall he speak: and he will shew you things to come. He shall glorify me: for he shall receive of mine, and shall shew it unto you" (John 16:12-14).

How does the Holy Spirit reveal these things to us? Usually, it is not by some vision or special experience but by the Word of God. As we study the Bible, the Spirit of God takes the Word and reveals the significance of its truths to us.

This, of course, is difficult for the world to understand. The unregenerate person usually is motivated by the desire to analyze and criticize the Bible rather than believe it. But the person who has been regenerated by receiving Jesus Christ as Saviour comes with an open heart, eager to learn more about God. Unless one accepts the Bible as the Word of God, he cannot glean the truths from it that God intends.

We must be very careful that we do not adopt the world's viewpoint and insist on having an intellectual understanding of the Bible before believing it. Knowing that it is God's Word, we are to accept what it says whether we can understand it or not. One's approach to the Scriptures is vitally important to his spiritual life. Schooling often greatly affects one's approach to the Scriptures. This is why I highly recommend Bible school training before university training. This was the order in which our children received their training, and we believe God has richly rewarded because of it. Some think a person needs a college education in order to understand the Bible, but that is not the case. It is important that a person be deeply grounded in the Word of God before he faces the humanistic, and even atheistic, philosophy of the world. It is better to have a knowledge of the Bible without a college education than a college education without a knowledge of the Bible.

Personal Responsibility

As the manna fell in the wilderness for the Israelites, each person was to gather what he needed. The Lord instructed, "Gather of it every man according to his eating, an omer for every man, according to the number of your persons; take ye every man for them which are in his tents" (Ex. 16:16). The Bible records that the Israelites "gathered every man according to his eating" (v. 18). From these statements we see that there was personal responsibility to gather the food that each one needed; some gathered more, others gathered less, but each was to gather according to his particular need.

Think of the parallel this has for our feeding on God's Word. Each one must gather spiritual food for himself. A believer cannot live on another person's experience. Testimonies are interesting, and it is wonderful to have a pastor who preaches good messages, but a believer cannot live on those things alone. Each Christian must gather his own spiritual food according to his own need. If each one is feeding himself individually, then the testimonies and messages of others will be of encouragement to him, and he will be of much encouragement to others.

How much appetite for the Word of God do you have? Do you come to the Word with a hungry heart to learn all you can in order that you might know God better? The more we learn about Him, the more we will want to learn. Since Christians are at different stages of spiritual growth, it is especially important that each one gather spiritual food according to his own need. As we come to God with open and believing hearts, He will provide spiritual food. He told the Israelites, "Open thy mouth wide, and I will fill it" (Ps. 81:10). Just as a mother bird feeds her young, so the Lord feeds us as we open our spiritual mouths for Him.

Have you wondered how long God kept providing manna for the Israelites? The answer is found in Exodus 16:35: "The children of Israel did eat manna forty years, until they came to a land inhabited; they did eat manna, until they came unto the borders of the land of Canaan." It is baffling to consider the quantity of manna it took to feed nearly three million people for one day alone. Yet God supplied this quantity every day for 40 years! This is another indication of God's inexhaustible supply. As Isaiah 40:8 says, "the grass withereth, the flower fadeth: but the word of our God shall stand for ever."

The Israelites continued to eat the manna until they came into the land of Canaan. Joshua 5:11,12 says, "They did eat of the old corn of the land on the morrow after the passover, unleavened cakes, and parched corn in the selfsame day. And the manna ceased on the morrow after they had eaten of the old corn of the land; neither had the children of Israel manna any more; but they did eat of the fruit of the land of Canaan that year."

Manna had served a special purpose during a given time in the life of the nation Israel, but after they came into the land, it was no longer needed. The Scofield Reference Bible has a significant note concerning the manna: "The manna is a type of Christ in humiliation, known 'after the flesh,' giving his flesh that the believer might have life (John 6. 49-51); while the 'old corn of the land' is Christ apprehended as risen, glorified, and seated in the heavenlies. Occupation with Christ on earth, 'crucified through weakness,' tends to a wilderness experience. An experience befitting the believer's place in the heavenlies demands an apprehension of the power of His resurrection (2 Cor. 5. 16; 13. 4; Phil. 3. 10; Eph. 1. 15-23). It is the contrast between 'milk' and 'meat' in Paul's writings (1 Cor. 3. 1,2; Heb. 5. 12-14; 6. 1-3)" (p. 263).

It is important that Christians progress from the milk stage of their spiritual lives to the meat stage. Hebrews 5:11-14 reveals that we grow spiritually stronger as we exercise our senses to discern good and evil. As we study God's Word and apply it to daily, life situations, we will mature in the Christian life.

Chapter 12

Water From the Rock

"And all the congregation of the children of Israel journeyed from the wilderness of Sin, after their journeys, according to the commandment of the Lord, and pitched in Rephidim: and there was no water for the people to drink" (Ex. 17:1).

Thirsty at Rephidim

Under the direction of God, Moses had led the Israelites into the wilderness where there was no food or water. Moses was persuaded that God could provide anything they needed. The testing that he had gone through earlier had persuaded him of God's ability to provide, so Moses gave unquestioned obedience when the Lord commanded the people to leave the wilderness of Sin and go to Rephidim. Notice that Exodus 17:1 says, "According to the commandment of the Lord." Moses was not acting on his own—he was under orders.

The Israelites had shown great confidence in Moses and in the Lord, as seen in Exodus 14:31, but this confidence soon waned when they faced the stark reality that there was no water. "Wherefore the people did chide with Moses, and said, Give us water that we may drink" (17:2). The people quarreled with Moses about the lack of water, but notice his response: "Why chide ye with me? Wherefore do ye tempt the Lord?" (v. 2). Moses immediately pointed to the real problem—the people were not trusting the Lord, even though earlier they had sung a song of assurance and praise to the Lord (Ex. 15).

Previously, the people had grumbled against Moses and against God because they had no food (16:3). Since God had miraculously provided at that time, one would hope they would have learned that God could and would provide any need they had. But when they faced a lack of water, they quarreled with Moses again.

The Israelites seemed to go through a certain cycle whenever they faced a difficult problem. They had a need, they grumbled, the need was miraculously met, but they seemed to lack thankfulness. As soon as the next need arose, they went through the same cycle again. Notice the divine commentary on the Israelites, as recorded in Psalm 78:11-20: "And they forgot His deeds, and His miracles that He had shown them. He wrought wonders before their fathers, in the land of Egypt, in the field of Zoan. He divided the sea, and caused them to pass through; and He made the waters stand up like a heap. Then He led them with the cloud by day, and all the night with a light of fire. He split the rocks in the wilderness, and gave them abundant drink like the ocean depths. He brought forth streams also from the rock, and caused waters to run down like rivers.

"Yet they still continued to sin against Him, to rebel against the Most High in the desert. And in their heart they put God to the test by asking food according to their desire. Then they spoke against God; they said, 'Can God prepare a table in the wilderness? Behold, He struck the rock, so that waters gushed out, and streams were overflowing; can He give bread also? Will He provide meat for His people?' " (NASB).

Rephidim was undoubtedly a barren place, and the Israelites desperately needed water. This serves as a reminder, however, that the believer also has needs which the world cannot supply. The Israelites were thirsting for actual water, but the believer's need is for the things of God. And Jesus promised to quench the believer's real thirst for spiritual truth: "Blessed are they which do hunger and thirst after righteousness: for they shall be filled" (Matt. 5:6). Isaiah exclaimed, "Ho, every one that thirsteth, come ye to the waters, and he that hath no money; come ye, buy, and eat; yea, come, buy wine and milk without money and without price" (Isa. 55:1). How refreshing it is to see a new Christian who is hungry and thirsty for the things of God.

Unfortunately, older Christians sometimes do not evidence this same desire, perhaps because the cares of this world have dulled this desire.

Questioning God

Moses made it clear that the Israelites were tempting God by arguing with him about water: "Moses said unto them, Why chide ye with me? Wherefore do ye tempt the Lord?" (Ex. 17:2). The people were not only questioning Moses as a leader, but they were also questioning God's goodness. "They tempted the Lord, saying, Is the Lord among us, or not?" (v. 7). This revealed the sad condition of their hearts. God had saved them from Egypt, had divided the Red Sea, had destroyed Egypt's power, had provided a cloud to guide and protect them and had given them manna to eat. Yet in the face of a new need they seemed to have forgotten all that God had previously done for them.

This teaches us the need of keeping our spiritual eyes fixed on Christ. When we face circumstances that seem impossible, we need to remind ourselves of all that Jesus Christ has done for us in the past. We need to be faithful in meditating on the Scriptures, which reveal the goodness and ability of God. Even though we don't know how our problem may be solved, we can be confident that there is a solution to the problem and that God will provide the answer. We should consider ourselves under the care of the Shepherd who is able to meet all of our needs. Such a concept of God led David to say, "The Lord is my shepherd; I shall not want" (Ps. 23:1).

God's supply of grace is sufficient for all of our needs. The Bible says, "God is able to make all grace abound toward you; that ye, always having all sufficiency in all things, may abound to every good work" (II Cor. 9:8). When there seems to be a lack, God may be testing us to see if we'll trust Him to supply what is needed.

Remember, God Himself led Israel to Rephidim; they were led there "according to the commandment of the Lord" (Ex. 17:1). Certainly God knew there was no water at Rephidim; this did not take Him by surprise. However, the Israelites blamed Moses and God as if neither one of them thought of this possibility.

When the believer faces some extremely difficult circumstances, he also has a tendency to blame others. Who do you blame at such times? The tendency is to say, or at least to think, "Why is God so hard on me?" or "Why did God let this happen to me?"

During Job's early experiences he was somewhat critical of God's ways, but he was finally able to say, "He knoweth the way that I take: when he hath tried me, I shall come forth as gold" (Job 23:10). Can you say that?

We need to realize, as did the writer of Proverbs, that "man's goings are of the Lord; how can a man then understand his own way?" (20:24). Even though we don't understand the circumstances we face, we should realize "that all things work together for good to them that love God, to them who are the called according to his purpose" (Rom. 8:28).

Moses' Reaction to Accusations

As the Israelites argued with Moses, he made it clear that they were arguing not just with him but also with God. That is why Moses said, "Why chide ye with me? Wherefore do ye tempt the Lord?" (Ex. 17:2). The word "tempt" means "to try" or "to test." They were trying God's patience by questioning His goodness and His faithfulness. Moses was God's appointed leader, and the Israelites were even accusing him of plotting to kill them by bringing them into the desert where there was no water (v. 3). Think of how this accusation must have crushed the heart of Moses. But anyone who is in the position of leadership must realize that he will be falsely accused at times by his followers.

When the Israelites accused Moses of plotting to kill them and their children, Moses did not try to defend himself. He "cried unto the Lord, saying, What shall I do unto this people? They be almost ready to stone me" (v. 4). Moses did not defend himself against the cruel accusations of the Israelites; he turned to God and sought His solution.

How refreshing it is to see the way Moses cast himself on the Lord rather than trying to defend himself. This is the biblical reaction prescribed for every believer when he is falsely accused. The Bible says, "Cast thy burden upon the Lord, and he shall sustain thee: he shall never suffer the righteous to be moved" (Ps. 55:22). How beautifully this ties in with the thought expressed in Psalm 37:5: "Commit thy way unto the Lord; trust also in him; and he shall bring it to pass."

Jesus Himself provided the example of how the believer should react: "Who, when he was reviled, reviled not again; when he suffered, he threatened not; but committed himself to him that judgeth righteously" (I Pet. 2:23). Although Jesus was an example to us, He is much more than that because He now indwells every believer and desires to express His characteristics through the believer. Believers are told, "Christ in you, the hope of glory" (Col. 1:27). Our hope of victory is in the indwelling Christ. As we live in fellowship with Jesus Christ, His characteristics will be revealed in and through our lives.

Moses' heart attitude toward God was revealed in that he "cried unto the Lord" (Ex. 17:4). Moses' acknowledgement of his own lack of ability is seen in his statement: "What shall I do unto this people?" (v. 4). But this statement also shows Moses' confidence in God's ability to solve the problem.

God's Response to Moses

How God responded to Moses is seen in verses 5,6: "And the Lord said unto Moses, Go on before the people, and take with thee of the elders of Israel; and thy rod, wherewith thou smotest the river, take in thine hand, and go. Behold, I will stand before thee there upon the rock in Horeb; and thou shalt smite the rock, and there shall come water out of it, that the people may drink." Moses' obedience is seen in the last statement of verse 6: "And Moses did so in the sight of the elders of Israel."

The need for water was about to be met because Moses went to God with the problem. The source of supply was God Himself.

God directed Moses to "the rock in Horeb" (v. 6). A rock was the last place that anyone would expect to find water, but God promised that water would come from the rock. But it wasn't just any rock; it might be called a "God-possessed rock" inasmuch as God said, "I will stand before thee there upon the rock in Horeb" (v. 6).

This rock clearly looked forward to the Lord Jesus Christ. This is evident from I Corinthians 10:4 which says that the Israelites "did all drink the same spiritual drink: for they drank of that spiritual Rock that followed them: and that Rock was Christ." In particular, the "rock in Horeb" (Ex. 17:6) represented the human nature of Christ, for He was smitten for our sins. Isaiah said, "Surely he hath borne our griefs, and carried our sorrows: yet we did esteem him stricken, smitten of God, and afflicted. But he was wounded for our transgressions, he was bruised for our iniquities: the chastisement of our peace was upon him; and with his stripes we are healed" (Isa. 53:4,5).

The source of help is God, as it was for the Israelites, but the channel is Jesus Christ.

The water which flowed from the rock suggests to us the Holy Spirit who came from the Father to indwell every believer. While Jesus was still on earth, He promised the disciples, "I will pray the Father, and he shall give you another Comforter, that he may abide with you for ever. . . . The Comforter, which is the Holy Ghost, whom the Father will send in my name, he shall teach you all things, and bring all things to your remembrance, whatsoever I have said unto you" (John 14:16,26). Jesus also told the disciples, "Nevertheless I tell you the truth; it is expedient for you that I go away: for if I go not away, the Comforter will not come unto you; but if I depart, I will send him unto you" (16:7). The Holy Spirit came from the Father to indwell believers after the Lord Jesus Christ had finished the work of redemption.

The Rock

Note the distinctions between the manna which God rained from heaven to provide food for the Israelites (Ex. 16:14) and the rock which was smitten to provide water (17:6). That both the manna and the rock point forward to Jesus Christ is evident from the New Testament (John 6:32,33; I Cor. 10:4). The manna points to the incarnation of Christ—His entering the world as a man (John 1:14). The smitten rock symbolizes His crucifixion—on the cross He was smitten of God for our sins (Isa. 53:4,5). Isaiah 53:10 says, "Yet it pleased the Lord to bruise him; he hath put him to grief: when thou shalt make his soul an offering for sin." Jesus Christ offered Himself as the sacrifice for sin so that anyone might have forgiveness of sin and eternal life by receiving Him as personal Saviour.

The water which flowed from the rock was a beautiful picture of the Holy Spirit who was given to believers after the Lord Jesus Christ was crucified and glorified. Jesus had promised that the Comforter would be sent (John 14:16), and on the Day of Pentecost the Holy Spirit came to indwell every believer (Acts 2:1-4). Just as Moses had to strike the rock before the water flowed, so the Lord Jesus had to be smitten for our sins and exalted at the right hand of the Father before the Holy Spirit was sent to indwell believers.

The Holy Spirit is often compared to water. Jesus said, "If any man thirst, let him come unto me, and drink. He that believeth on me, as the scripture hath said, out of his belly shall flow rivers of living water" (John 7:37,38). Jesus spoke these words before He ascended to heaven; thus, verse 39 says, "(But this spake he of the Spirit, which they that believe on him should receive: for the Holy Ghost was not yet given; because that Jesus was not yet glorified.)"

So we see that running water was used to illustrate the ministry of the Spirit. This was no doubt what Christ had in mind when He told the woman at the well, "If thou knewest the gift of God, and who it is that saith to thee, Give me to drink; thou wouldest have asked of him, and he would have given thee living water. . . . Whosoever drinketh of the water that I shall give him shall never thirst; but the water that I shall give him shall be in him a well of water springing up into everlasting life" (4:10,14).

Three of the five types of the death of Christ have now been presented in the Book of Exodus. The Passover told of redemption by blood from the penalty of sin. The passing through the Red Sea (a figure of participating in death) symbolized redemption by power from the slavery of sin. And the smitten rock illustrated the new life provided in Christ through the Holy Spirit. Thus, both Calvary and Pentecost are pictured in the Old Testament types, and these two events must always be thought of in relation to each other.

Characteristics of God's Provision

The water flowing from the rock indicates the provision for life. The psalmist said, "Behold, he smote the rock, that the waters gushed out, and the streams overflowed" (Ps. 78:20). The smitten rock pointed to the smitten Christ who paid the penalty of sin. The gushing streams of water picture the gracious supply of life through the Holy Spirit.

God smote His Son and raised Him from the dead, thereby sending forth the life-giving stream, but man must come and drink. Although Jesus Christ has paid the penalty of sin for all (I John 2:2), only those who personally receive Him as Saviour have forgiveness of sin and eternal life (John 1:12; 5:24).

When God provides, He provides abundantly. When God provided water for the Israelites, the psalmist said, "He opened the rock and the waters gushed out; they ran in the dry places like a river" (Ps. 105:41). Concerning the life which the Lord Jesus Christ provides, He said, "I am come that they might have life, and that they might have it more abundantly" (John 10:10). This coincides with the way Jesus compared the Spirit to the abundance of running water (John 4:14; 7:37,38). So the rock in the wilderness prefigured Jesus Christ.

The constant provision for the Israelites is emphasized in I Corinthians 10:4: "They drank of that spiritual Rock that followed them: and that Rock was Christ." Notice that the Rock "followed them." Their needs were taken care of by God's abundant provision.

Not only was the supply abundant, but it was also free. All the Israelites had to do was to partake of what had been provided. This is a reminder of Isaiah's statement: "Ho, every one that thirsteth, come ye to the waters, and he that hath no money; come ye, buy, and eat; yea, come, buy wine and milk without money and without price" (Isa. 55:1). Jesus emphasized to the woman at the well that the water He provided was free: "If thou knewest the gift of God, and who it is that saith to thee, Give me to drink; thou wouldest have

asked of him, and he would have given thee living water"
(John 4:10). The free access to the water is also emphasized
in Revelation 22:17: "And the Spirit and the bride say,
Come. And let him that heareth say, Come. And let him that
is athirst come. And whosoever will, let him take the water of
life freely."

It is also significant to observe that God's supply is
always near. The Israelites did not have to go a long distance
to receive water; God directed them to a source in their area.
So also, God's spiritual supply is always near. Romans 10:8
says, "The word is nigh thee, even in thy mouth, and in thy
heart: that is, the word of faith, which we preach." Verse 13
states, "For whosoever shall call upon the name of the Lord
shall be saved."

There was no excuse for the Israelites' not having
sufficient water, because as I Corinthians 10:4 indicates, the
Rock followed them. The supply was always accessible to
them. So also, even though the Lord Jesus Christ died for sin
nearly 2000 years ago, what He accomplished is just as
powerful and available now as it was immediately after His
death on the cross. The invitation for all to come and to
drink freely still stands (Rev. 22:17). And remember the
promise of the Lord Jesus: "All that the Father giveth me
shall come to me; and him that cometh to me I will in no
wise cast out" (John 6:37). All are invited to come. Jesus
said, "Come unto me, all ye that labour and are heavy laden,
and I will give you rest" (Matt. 11:28). And what a
wonderful promise we have in Isaiah 1:18: "Come now, and
let us reason together, saith the Lord: though your sins be as
scarlet, they shall be as white as snow; though they be red
like crimson, they shall be as wool."

First Corinthians 10:4 reveals that the Israelites all drank
of the Rock that followed them. This is a beautiful illustration of the fact that during the Church Age every believer
is made a partaker of the Holy Spirit. Believers are told, "For
by one Spirit are we all baptized into one body, whether we
be Jews or Gentiles, whether we be bond or free; and have
been all made to drink into one Spirit" (I Cor. 12:13). It is
important to realize that every believer has the Spirit of God.
It is not possible to maintain that a person can receive Christ
as Saviour at one point in time and not receive the Holy

Spirit until another point in time. The Bible reveals that every believer has the Spirit of God. Romans 8:9 says, "Ye are not in the flesh, but in the Spirit, if so be that the Spirit of God dwell in you. Now if any man have not the Spirit of Christ, he is none of his."

The Holy Spirit: Receiving and Filling

Receiving the Holy Spirit does not depend on our attainment, or work, but on Christ's finished work. That is why John 1:12 says, "As many as received him, to them gave he power to become the sons of God, even to them that believe on his name."

To drink of the one Spirit is the birthright and the heritage of every born-again person. It is important to realize, however, that although every believer has the Spirit of God, not every believer is filled with the Holy Spirit. Receiving the Spirit is the believer's heritage. Ephesians 1:13,14 says, "In whom [Christ] ye also trusted, after that ye heard the word of truth, the gospel of your salvation: in whom also after that ye [literally, having] believed, ye were sealed with the holy Spirit of promise, which is the earnest of our inheritance until the redemption of the purchased possession, unto the praise of his glory." From these verses and from Romans 8:9 we learn that every believer has the Holy Spirit because he is sealed with the Holy Spirit. Ephesians 4:30 reveals that the believer is sealed with the Holy Spirit "unto the day of redemption."

Whereas receiving the Holy Spirit is the believer's heritage, being filled with the Holy Spirit is both the believer's privilege and command. The Bible says, "Be not drunk with wine, wherein is excess; but be filled with the Spirit" (5:18). The filling here referred to is the control of the Holy Spirit. Every believer, because he has the Holy Spirit indwelling him, is exhorted to let the Holy Spirit control all of his life.

The life through the Holy Spirit is the same in all believers, but the manifestation of that life in terms of spiritual development and spiritual maturity is different in each believer.

Every person who has been born again by receiving Christ as Saviour has the life of Christ in him by means of the Holy Spirit. Therefore, such terms as "deeper life" or "higher life" are sometimes misleading because all believers have the same spiritual life. However, this life can, and does, develop differently in different believers. Every believer has a varying degree of spiritual maturity. Although a baby may be physically complete when it is born, it needs to grow to physical maturity. So also, a believer in Christ has complete life when he is born again, but he needs to grow to spiritual maturity.

Those Christians who are more concerned about pleasing themselves than about pleasing Christ are carnal Christians. Paul told the Corinthians, "And I, brethren, could not speak unto you as unto spiritual, but as unto carnal, even as unto babes in Christ. I have fed you with milk, not with meat: for hitherto ye were not able to bear it, neither yet now are ye able. For ye are yet carnal: for whereas there is among you envying, and strife, and divisions, are ye not carnal, and walk as men?" (I Cor. 3:1-3). The spiritual person allows the Holy Spirit to fill, or control, his life (Eph. 5:18-20).

There is no difference in character as far as life itself is concerned; the only difference is in the development and growth of that life, which is determined by the individual believer. The one who grows to maturity is the one who has his senses exercised by taking the Word of God and applying it to daily life situations (Heb. 5:13,14).

Thus, the need of each person who knows Jesus Christ as Saviour is to obey the injunction to "be filled with the Spirit" (Eph. 5:18) and to "walk in the Spirit, and ye shall not fulfil the lust of the flesh" (Gal. 5:16).

Chapter 13

Spiritual Conflict

After recording the incident of obtaining water from the rock, the Bible says, "Then came Amalek, and fought with Israel in Rephidim" (Ex. 17:8).

Israel's First Warfare

This was Israel's first involvement in warfare. After they had tasted of the heavenly food (manna) and after they had drunk from the rock, the warfare began. The same thing happens in a believer's life after Christ has His rightful place in that person's heart and the Holy Spirit has been given His rightful place of control. In other words, after the believer has tasted spiritual food and drunk of the spiritual Rock, spiritual warfare begins in his life also.

When warfare came to Israel, the people were resting in Rephidim. This is a reminder that when we are at rest in the Lord because of the salvation we have in Him through the power of the Holy Spirit, we need to watch for the Enemy. After the new and holy nature of Christ is implanted in our hearts, Satan is ready to do battle with us.

Some people are under the impression that receiving Jesus Christ as Saviour ends any conflict in their lives. However, it is really only the beginning. Before receiving Christ as Saviour, a person has only one nature—the old, or Adamic, nature. There is no conflict as long as a person has only one nature to satisfy. But upon trusting Christ as Saviour, a person receives a new and holy nature which is in immediate conflict with the old nature. This conflict is referred to in Galatians 5:17: "For the flesh [old nature]

124

lusteth against the Spirit, and the Spirit against the flesh: and these are contrary the one to the other: so that ye cannot do the things that ye would." However, the preceding verse shows the way of victory for the Christian: "Walk in the Spirit, and ye shall not fulfil the lust of the flesh" (v. 16).

Until the Israelites met Amalek, they had little conflict. They had not fought with Pharaoh in Egypt nor did they break the power of Egypt at the Red Sea by submerging Pharaoh and his army in the water. God had done all of this in their behalf, even though individual Israelites were not faithful in believing Him.

So also, Christ has won all the battles for us and has obtained our peace. In Him there is forgiveness of sin. He alone died on the cross, was laid in the tomb and arose from the dead to accomplish our justification. He overcame Satan and took away the sting of death. These things were all accomplished apart from any of our activity.

The Book of Hebrews tells of that which Christ accomplished for us: "When he [Christ] had by himself purged our sins, sat down on the right hand of the Majesty on high" (1:3). The defeat of Satan is mentioned in Hebrews 2:14: "Forasmuch then as the children are partakers of flesh and blood, he [Christ] also himself likewise took part of the same; that through death he might destroy him that had the power of death, that is, the devil."

Because of what Christ has accomplished for us, Ephesians 1:3 says, "Blessed be the God and Father of our Lord Jesus Christ, who hath blessed us with all spiritual blessings in heavenly places in Christ."

In Israel's case, all previous conflicts had been between Jehovah and the Enemy, Satan. All the Israelites had to do was to stand still and see and enjoy the fruits of victory. But now they were about to enter serious conflict.

The moment the believer discovers and appropriates the truth concerning the personality and power of the Holy Spirit (as symbolized by the water from the smitten rock), he suddenly becomes aware of the new Enemy symbolized by Amalek.

Amalek's fighting against Israel parallels the struggle an individual believer has because of his two natures. Were there only darkness (the old nature) there would be no conflict.

Were there only light (the new nature) there would be no conflict. But because the believer has both natures, there is a constant struggle between the two. The statement in Galatians 5:17 which says, "The flesh lusteth against the Spirit, and the Spirit against the flesh" means that the desires of these two natures are totally opposed to each other. That is why the Christian experiences a constant struggle in life. He must choose which desires he will yield to—the desires of the new nature or the desires of the old nature.

Exodus 17:8 indicates the first time that Israel was really engaged in conflict with an enemy: "Then came Amalek, and fought with Israel in Rephidim." They were experiencing something they had not known before. They may have thought that once they were delivered from Egypt they would never experience conflict, but what a lesson they had to learn!

Receiving the New Nature

In the case of the Christian, God does not change a person's nature. Many teach that God changes a person's nature so that after he receives Christ as Saviour he will always be a complete victor over sin. But a changed nature is not taught in scripture. God does not improve or overhaul the old nature. Nothing is done to the old nature—God leaves it as it is. What He does, however, is to give man a new nature when he is born again. God does not attempt to improve the weaknesses of the old nature; He gives the believer an entirely new nature. So God does not remove man's old nature; rather, He adds the new nature. This new nature is "born . . . of the Spirit" (John 3:5). Believers are "partakers of the divine nature" (II Pet. 1:4).

The new life is Christ Himself, not the old life made over. And the wonderful truth is, "He that hath the Son hath life," but the sobering truth is, "He that hath not the Son of God hath not life" (I John 5:12).

At the time of salvation a divine nature is communicated to the believer. This divine nature is created within the believer by the Holy Spirit through the Word of God. The Bible refers to Christians as "being born again, not of corruptible seed, but of incorruptible, by the word of God, which liveth and abideth for ever" (I Pet. 1:23). Thus we see that the word "seed" is used in reference to the new nature. First John 3:9 also uses the word "seed": "Whosoever is born of God doth not commit sin; for his seed remaineth in him: and he cannot sin, because he is born of God." This seed is pure and is not capable of sin.

Although a new nature is implanted in the believer at the time of salvation, the old nature, or sin nature, remains unchanged until death or until Christ returns to catch away the believer from the earth. The Apostle Paul told of this in I Corinthians 15:51-53: "Behold, I shew you a mystery; We shall not all sleep, but we shall all be changed, in a moment, in the twinkling of an eye, at the last trump: for the trumpet shall sound, and the dead shall be raised incorruptible, and we shall be changed. For this corruptible must put on incorruption, and this mortal must put on immortality."

So in every Christian there are two natures, one sinful and one sinless. One is born of the flesh (after Adam), the other is born of God. These two natures differ from each other in origin, character, disposition and in the activities they produce. The two natures have absolutely nothing in common and are in complete opposition to each other.

Illustrations of the Two Natures

It is important to identify exactly who Amalek was, because it is significant that the Lord used him to symbolize the believer's old nature. From Genesis 36:12 we learn that Amalek was the grandson of Esau. Esau was the twin brother of Jacob, and because Esau was born first, he had rightful claim to the birthright. But he sold his birthright for some pottage. The birthright involved not only physical aspects but also spiritual aspects. The property to be inherited was the physical part; the spiritual leadership the oldest son was to exercise was the spiritual part. There were no priests at the time Jacob and Esau lived; the oldest son in the family was to carry out this responsibility for his family. So we see the full significance of what Esau was willing to give up for food when he was desperately hungry. He, too, is a significant illustration of the flesh, or the old nature.

The New Testament refers to Esau as an example not to be followed. Hebrews 12:16,17 says, "Lest there be any fornicator, or profane person, as Esau, who for one morsel of meat sold his birthright. For ye know how that afterward, when he would have inherited the blessing, he was rejected: for he found no place of repentance, though he sought it carefully with tears." This is a picture of the corruptness of the old nature.

On the other hand, Jacob sought the things of God, especially the birthright. True, he went after it in a carnal way, but when God had won over his carnality, he became "Israel"—a prince with God. Thus, Esau represents the old nature, and Jacob represents the new nature. These two are in constant conflict.

Other people also illustrate the two natures—for instance, Abraham's two sons Ishmael and Isaac. Ishmael was born after the flesh. God had promised Abraham many descendants, but after waiting for some time, Abraham had no son. Abraham's wife, Sarah, suggested an alternate plan. She gave her handmaid to Abraham, and a child, who was named Ishmael, was conceived and born. As long as Ishmael was alone in the house, there was no struggle, but when Isaac, the son of promise, was later born to Abraham and Sarah, conflict arose in the family. The New Testament comments concerning the conflict between these two sons: "But as then he that was born after the flesh persecuted him that was born after the Spirit, even so it is now" (Gal. 4:29). These two could not live in harmony together because one was born of a bondwoman and the other was born of a freewoman. God's solution is seen in His instructions to Abraham: "Cast out the bondwoman and her son: for the son of the bondwoman shall not be heir with the son of the freewoman" (v. 30).

The conflict of the two natures is also seen in the life of the Apostle Paul. After presenting the significant truths of Romans 5 and 6, Paul explained in Romans 7 the turmoil he went through as he struggled with the conflict between the desires of the new nature and the desires of the old nature. Paul constantly referred to himself in this chapter—personal pronouns occur many times. This reveals that he tried to solve his inner battle by relying on self. The Holy Spirit is not mentioned once in Romans 7.

However, in Romans 8 Paul presented victory in the Holy Spirit. The Holy Spirit is mentioned 19 times in this chapter. Read Romans 5—8 and notice the development within the chapters.

The two names given to Jacob also remind us of the two natures of the believer. Jacob was his name when he lived after the flesh. Later, when he began to live for God, his name was changed to Israel, which means "prince with God." A play on these names is made in Isaiah 9:8: "The Lord sends a message against Jacob, and it falls on Israel" (NASB). Inasmuch as Jacob's name was changed to Israel, his sons and their descendants became known as the children of Israel.

Pharaoh and Amalek are also a reminder of two different powers that influence the Christian's life. Pharaoh is a reminder of Satan, because he tried to keep the Israelites in slavery, just as Satan tries to keep people enslaved to sin. Amalek, on the other hand, is a reminder of the flesh, or old nature, for just as Amalek fought to keep Israel from victory, so the flesh seeks to keep the Christian from victory.

Pharaoh hindered Israel's deliverance from Egypt, and Amalek hindered Israel's progress once they were delivered from Egypt. Satan seeks to keep people in bondage and tries to prevent them from receiving Jesus Christ as Saviour. Once a person receives Christ as Saviour, however, the flesh opposes spiritual victory.

Two Aspects of Victory

Remember, Israel did not attack Amalek, Amalek attacked Israel. The new nature delights in God—it loves to commune with Him and to feed on His Word. But the old nature gives no peace to the believer. It robs him of joy and opposes everything that is of the Spirit. But when the flesh battles against the believer as Amalek fought against the Israelites, the Holy Spirit takes up the battle in behalf of the believer.

As Amalek attacked the Israelites, God revealed a means of victory for His people: "Moses said unto Joshua, Choose us out men, and go out, fight with Amalek: to morrow I will stand on the top of the hill with the rod of God in mine hand. So Joshua did as Moses had said to him, and fought

with Amalek: and Moses, Aaron, and Hur went up to the top
of the hill. And it came to pass, when Moses held up his
hand, that Israel prevailed: and when he let down his hand,
Amalek prevailed. But Moses' hands were heavy; and they
took a stone, and put it under him, and he sat thereon; and
Aaron and Hur stayed up his hands, the one on the one side,
and the other on the other side; and his hands were steady
until the going down of the sun. And Joshua discomfited
[overwhelmed] Amalek and his people with the edge of the
sword" (Ex. 17:9-13).

Israel's source of victory had two aspects—warfare and
intercession. The warfare took place in the valley, which
reminds us of the valley of everyday life. The real warfare
takes place as we stand on the side of Christ against the
downward pull of the old nature. We must determine to put
our lives at His disposal for His use, and we must determine
that our lives will be godly and pleasing to Him.

Joshua, the man of the Spirit, took his stand against the
enemy. Amalek, an illustration of the flesh, took his stand
against God's people.

The Christian life is one of warfare, but it is a spiritual
warfare. Ephesians 6:12-18 tells of this spiritual warfare.
Verse 17 tells believers, "Take the helmet of salvation, and
the sword of the Spirit, which is the word of God." In
addition to taking the armor of God, the believer is to be
"praying always with all prayer and supplication in the Spirit,
and watching thereunto with all perseverance and
supplication for all saints" (v. 18). The two aspects of the
spiritual warfare are evident—Joshua with the sword (of the
Spirit, or the Word) and Moses with uplifted hands of
intercession and prayer.

Although there was warfare between Amalek and the
Israelites in the valley, the real battle was on the hilltop
where Moses interceded. As long as Moses' hands were
extended in prayer toward heaven, the Israelites had the
advantage in the battle. But when his hands became heavy
and were lowered, the battle went in favor of Amalek and his
army.

The respective actions of Moses on the hilltop and Joshua
in the valley revealed the provisions God has made for us to
combat the flesh. We have the comfort of knowing that we

are pronounced victorious and truly established as victors even before we enter the field of conflict. May we by faith approach the battle, singing the victor's song and appropriate the victory He has already won for us. The following verses tell of this victory: "But thanks be to God, which giveth us the victory through our Lord Jesus Christ" (I Cor. 15:57). "Now thanks be unto God, which always causeth us to triumph in Christ, and maketh manifest the savour of his knowledge by us in every place" (II Cor. 2:14). (See also Eph. 6:13 and Rom. 8:37.) How wonderful it is to realize that Jesus Christ provides all that we need to be victorious in spiritual warfare through the Holy Spirit.

Source of Victory

From the battle between Amalek and the Israelites we can learn many spiritual lessons. Amalek is a type of the old nature. The old nature is not eradicated when a person receives Christ as Saviour, but it is to be totally subjected. It is brought into subjection, just as Israel had victory over Amalek, through warfare and through intercessory prayer.

Joshua fought in the valley—a picture of the everyday warfare of the Christian life—while Moses interceded on the hilltop. Previously the Israelites had eaten the manna (the symbol of the Word of God) and had drunk the water from the rock (a symbol of the Holy Spirit). So, too, the believer must meditate on the Word of God and rely on the Spirit before he can expect spiritual victory.

As Joshua fought with Amalek and his men, he used the sword mightily. The Bible says, "Joshua discomfited Amalek and his people with the edge of the sword" (Ex. 17:13). Joshua's use of the sword is a reminder that the believer wins spiritual victories by using the sword of the Spirit. The Bible tells believers, "Take the helmet of salvation, the sword of the Spirit, which is the word of God" (Eph. 6:17). But while the believer is engaged in spiritual warfare, he is also to be "praying always with all prayer and supplication in the Spirit" (v. 18).

The combination of Moses' intercession on the hilltop and Joshua's fighting in the valley resulted in victory for the Israelites. They had to fight before they could be pronounced victors, whereas believers are already pronounced victors over sin because of what Jesus Christ accomplished for them. Their responsibility is to appropriate by faith the victory that Christ has made available to them. Ephesians 6:13 says, "Wherefore take unto you the whole armour of God, that ye may be able to withstand in the evil day, and having done all, to stand." This verse views the believer as being victorious in spiritual warfare, and he is to stand as a victor.

Romans 8:37 assures believers, "We are more than conquerors through him that loved us." Jesus has already won the battle for us, so we must realize that we are already victors and appropriate this victory by faith. If we do not realize that we are already victors, we will flounder in the Christian life as Paul did (see Rom. 7). When we realize, however, that victory has been provided and the Holy Spirit will enable us to participate in it, we will be able to say with Paul, "For the law of the Spirit of life in Christ Jesus hath made me free from the law of sin and death" (Rom. 8:2).

Appropriating Victory

However, the believer is not to be completely passive in spiritual warfare. Some think they are to do nothing but are to let God do everything. Victory does come from God, but He expects the believer to be involved in appropriating the victory. It is not sufficient that Moses interceded on the hilltop; Joshua had to be fighting down in the valley. So also, Galatians 5:16 tells believers, "Walk in the Spirit, and ye shall not fulfil the lust of the flesh." God provides, but man must appropriate the victory—he must go out and get it.

It is a principle with God that although He foreordains victory for His own, He requires that they appropriate the victory. For instance, He had promised the Israelites the land of Canaan, but they had to actually go into the land and take it for themselves. God said to Joshua, "Every place that the sole of your foot shall tread upon, that have I given unto you, as I said unto Moses" (Josh. 1:3). God had given the land to the Israelites, but they had to go in and possess it.

This principle of faith is seen in the battle between the Israelites and Amalek and his people. Both elements are stated in Exodus 17:10: "So Joshua did as Moses had said to him, and fought with Amalek: and Moses, Aaron, and Hur went up to the top of the hill." Actual combat along with intercessory prayer brought victory for Israel.

As long as Moses' hands were extended to heaven in intercession, the Israelites experienced victory in the valley. But when his arms became tired and his hands lowered, the battle went against the Israelites. Verse 12 reveals how Moses was helped in this matter: "But Moses' hands were heavy; and they took a stone, and put it under him, and he sat thereon; and Aaron and Hur stayed up his hands, the one on the one side, and the other on the other side; and his hands were steady until the going down of the sun."

Although in this particular instance Moses' hands were extended to heaven, this is not necessarily the posture one should always assume in praying. This was a common posture throughout Bible times, but the important matter in praying is one's heart attitude, not his physical posture. This incident in the life of Israel was for the purpose of teaching them that the victory belonged to God alone. They were not to glory in their own numbers and strength but were to glory in God.

Joshua and Moses illustrate what the believer is to do in spiritual warfare. Joshua is a picture of a Spirit-filled man who fights in the front-line attack. He used the sword just as the believer should use the sword of the Spirit. But fighting alone is not enough; there must be intercessory prayer. Moses is a picture of the Spirit-filled man who is on good praying terms with God.

Satan's Opposition

Satan opposes praying, so he will oppose the praying person first and foremost. Satan realizes that prayer is the key to total victory. The real battle between Israel and Amalek took place on the hilltop as Moses interceded for Israel. His arms became tired, and it's also possible for the believer to grow weary in the battle of intercession. On some days it seems so hard for the believer to spend time in prayer. Satan can do many things to disturb our prayer life, and if he can keep us from praying, he certainly will, since he knows that is how spiritual battles are won.

Although we grow weary in the battle of supplication, Luke 18:1 exhorts us, "Men ought always to pray, and not to faint." We tire so easily in the serious business of intercessory prayer. And remember, it was no different when Jesus was on earth with the disciples. As He was contemplating going to the cross, He left His disciples in one spot while He moved a little distance away from them to talk to His heavenly Father. When He returned to the disciples, Jesus found them asleep. He said to them, "Could ye not watch with me one hour? Watch and pray, that ye enter not into temptation: the spirit indeed is willing, but the flesh is weak" (Matt. 26:40,41).

Notice that it was a battle between the Spirit and the flesh—"the spirit indeed is willing, but the flesh is weak" (v. 41). This is the same battle mentioned in Galatians 5:17: "For the flesh lusteth against the Spirit, and the Spirit against the flesh: and these are contrary the one to the other." Because of the seriousness of the spiritual battle, believers are told, "Pray without ceasing" (I Thess. 5:17). This is the way spiritual battles are won, but we often sadly fail. Our hearts, our bodies and our minds grow weary so easily. Remember, as soon as we forsake our dependency on God, the flesh prevails.

But there is encouraging news concerning weariness in prayer. Moses became weary as he interceded for Israel, but Aaron and Hur willingly and ably helped him. Aaron was later established as the head of Israel's priesthood, so this incident speaks plainly of the high priest and his intercessory responsibilities. We, too, have a High Priest in the heavenlies who is making intercession for us—the Lord Jesus Christ. Hebrews 7:25 says of Him, "Wherefore he is able also to save them to the uttermost that come unto God by him, seeing he ever liveth to make intercession for them." So even while the believer is interceding for others, the Lord Jesus Christ is interceding for him. This gives us the spiritual strength we need as we pray and as we enter spiritual warfare.

Not only is the Lord Jesus Christ interceding for us, but also the Holy Spirit enables us to pray as we should. Hur, at Moses' side and supporting one of his arms, is a good illustration of this fact. Romans 8:26 says, "Likewise the Spirit also helpeth our infirmities: for we know not what we should pray for as we ought: but the Spirit itself maketh intercession for us with groanings which cannot be uttered." This reveals what the Holy Spirit does for us as He strives against the flesh (Gal. 5:17). Romans 8:27 says of the Holy Spirit, "He that searcheth the hearts knoweth what is the mind of the Spirit, because he maketh intercession for the saints according to the will of God." What an encouraging truth this is!

Every believer should be encouraged when he realizes that the Holy Spirit is helping him to pray as he should and that the Lord Jesus Christ is interceding in heaven before the Father. Jesus Christ especially intercedes for us when we sin. First John 2:1 says, "My little children, these things write I unto you, that ye sin not. And if any man sin, we have an advocate with the Father, Jesus Christ the righteous." Because of what the Lord Jesus Christ accomplished for us when He died on the cross, He is able to intercede in our behalf. The shedding of His blood paid the complete penalty for sin.

Prayer and God's Word

Joshua and his activity completes the typical picture of the battle array. Exodus 17:13 says, "Joshua discomfited Amalek and his people with the edge of the sword." This was accomplished because Moses was on the hilltop, assisted by Aaron and Hur as he interceded for Joshua and the Israelites.

We, too, can do battle against the old nature when we use the sword as Joshua did. Whereas Joshua used an actual sword, we are to use "the sword of the Spirit, which is the word of God" (Eph. 6:17). Our battle is primarily against the old nature, because Satan usually approaches us through the desires of our old nature. As we fortify ourselves with the Word of God and use the sword of the Spirit, we will have victory over the old nature.

Hebrews 4:12 reveals how effective the Word of God is: "For the word of God is quick [living], and powerful, and sharper than any twoedged sword, piercing even to the dividing asunder of soul and spirit, and of the joints and marrow, and is a discerner of the thoughts and intents of the heart." Thus, the Word of God is an effective weapon. So as we engage in spiritual warfare, we must remember that it is not by prayer alone and it is not by the use of the sword alone that we win spiritual battles. But by using both of these weapons together, we can experience victory.

It is important to have the Word of God stored in one's heart. The psalmist said, "Thy word have I hid in mine heart, that I might not sin against thee" (Ps. 119:11). The Word of God has a highly significant part in the things accomplished in each believer. Jesus told His followers, "Now ye are clean through the word which I have spoken unto you" (John 15:3). In His prayer to the heavenly Father, Jesus said, "Sanctify them through thy truth: thy word is truth" (17:17). God's Word is now available to us in written form. God reveals Himself to us in the Bible. If anyone wants to know Jesus Christ better, he must know the Bible better.

Through the Bible we learn of our position in Jesus Christ and what He accomplished for us when He died in our place. As we learn what Jesus Christ has done for us, we are then responsible to live accordingly. Proper doctrine determines proper living. Thus, Romans 6:3-6 reveals what we are to know; verse 11 reveals that we are to count on it by an act of faith; verses 12 and 13 reveal that we are to present ourselves to the Lord to carry out His will in us. This presentation of ourselves is a result of what we know and count on. This is all accomplished through the Holy Spirit. Romans 8:13 says, "For if ye live after the flesh, ye shall die: but if ye through the Spirit do mortify the deeds of the body, ye shall live." The Holy Spirit enables the believer to live in victory over sin as he puts the acts of flesh to death by saying no to sin and expecting the Holy Spirit to accomplish the victory.

Potential Victory

Remember that every believer has a sin nature as well as a new nature, so sin dwells in him, but it is not to reign supreme in his life. This is why Romans 6:12 says, "Let not sin therefore reign in your mortal body, that ye should obey it in the lusts thereof." And verse 14 adds, "For sin shall not have dominion over you: for ye are not under the law, but under grace." So while sin still dwells in the believer, it is not to reign in him.

Potential victory has been provided in Jesus Christ, but we must enter into the warfare and claim the victory for ourselves. This is done by an act of faith. The pastor who baptized me reminded me of an especially meaningful verse concerning this matter: "Fight the good fight of faith, lay hold on eternal life, whereunto thou art also called, and hast professed a good profession before many witnesses" (I Tim. 6:12). At the end of his life the Apostle Paul was able to say, "I have fought a good fight, I have finished my course, I have kept the faith" (II Tim. 4:7). Are you able to say that? You can be if you heed the instructions of Ephesians 6:11: "Put on the whole armour of God, that ye may be able to stand against the wiles of the devil."

In realizing the need for us to appropriate the victory Christ has provided, it is encouraging to see what Paul had to say. On the one hand he said, "O wretched man that I am! Who shall deliver me from the body of this death?" (Rom. 7:24). But on the other hand, he was able to triumphantly say, "I thank God through Jesus Christ our Lord" (v. 25). Paul realized that victory came by means of Jesus Christ.

Spiritual victory is possible for a believer as he knows Jesus Christ—the source of victory—and trusts Him. The Bible says, "Whatsoever is born of God overcometh the world: and this is the victory that overcometh the world, even our faith" (I John 5:4). By faith we trust Jesus Christ as personal Saviour, and this relationship with Him becomes the basis of spiritual victory as we believe Him for it. Thus, we can stand fearlessly against the Enemy. Faith is the victory—"Thanks be to God, which giveth us the victory through our Lord Jesus Christ" (I Cor. 15:57).

As Moses interceded for Joshua, who was battling Amalek in the valley, his "hands were heavy; and they took a stone, and put it under him, and he sat thereon; and Aaron and Hur stayed up his hands, the one on the one side, and the other on the other side; and his hands were steady until the going down of the sun" (Ex. 17:12).

Although Moses' arms wavered, we are not to waver in what we ask of the Lord. The Bible says, "If any of you lack wisdom, let him ask of God, that giveth to all men liberally, and upbraideth not; and it shall be given him. Let him ask in faith, nothing wavering. For he that wavereth is like a wave of the sea driven with the wind and tossed. For let not that man think that he shall receive any thing of the Lord" (James 1:5-7). In coming to the Lord, we are not to waver, but we are to "believe that he is, and that he is a rewarder of them that diligently seek him" (Heb. 11:6).

Whereas unsteady hands receive nothing, the promises of God never produce unsteadiness. The Bible says, "Hast thou not known? Hast thou not heard, that the everlasting God, the Lord, the Creator of the ends of the earth, fainteth not, neither is weary? There is no searching of his understanding. He giveth power to the faint; and to them that have no might he increaseth strength" (Isa. 40:28,29).

As Amalek fought against Joshua and the Israelites, God made a final decree against him. Exodus 17:13-16 reveals what was involved in this decree: "And Joshua discomfited Amalek and his people with the edge of the sword. And the Lord said unto Moses, Write this for a memorial in a book, and rehearse it in the ears of Joshua: for I will utterly put out the remembrance of Amalek from under heaven. And Moses built an altar, and called the name of it Jehovah-nissi: for he said: Because the Lord hath sworn that the Lord will have war with Amalek from generation to generation."

Notice especially verse 16: "The Lord hath sworn that the Lord will have war with Amalek from generation to generation." In the Christian warfare, which is a segment of the battle of the ages, there must be no compromise. We cannot afford to spare the flesh, the old nature. Paul said, "I know that in me (that is, in my flesh,) dwelleth no good thing" (Rom. 7:18). Because there is nothing good in the old nature, Paul told believers, "Put ye on the Lord Jesus Christ, and make not provision for the flesh, to fulfil the lusts thereof" (13:14).

Ultimatum Against the Flesh

God's decree against the flesh is one of death. Colossians 3:5-10 tells believers what God wants them to do concerning the flesh, or old nature: "Mortify therefore your members which are upon the earth; fornication, uncleanness, inordinate affection, evil concupiscence, and covetousness, which is idolatry: for which things' sake the wrath of God cometh on the children of disobedience: in the which ye also walked some time, when ye lived in them. But now ye also put off all these; anger, wrath, malice, blasphemy, filthy communication out of your mouth. Lie not one to another, seeing that ye have put off the old man with his deeds; and have put on the new man, which is renewed in knowledge after the image of him that created him."

The old nature cannot be reformed, corrected or altered in any way. It is totally depraved; it can do nothing that pleases God. The Bible says, "The carnal mind is enmity against God: for it is not subject to the law of God, neither indeed can be" (Rom. 8:7).

Although God makes no attempt to change the old nature, He has made a way for the believer to have victory over it. God gives the Holy Spirit to us at the time of salvation, and by relying on Him, we experience victory over the desires of the old nature. Galatians 5:16,17 says, "Walk in the Spirit, and ye shall not fulfil the lust of the flesh. For the flesh lusteth against the Spirit, and the Spirit against the flesh: and these are contrary the one to the other: so that ye cannot do the things that ye would." So there is victory through the Holy Spirit as the believer yields to Him.

The Bible tells of the victory the believer can expect: "Thanks be unto God, which always causeth us to triumph in Christ" (II Cor. 2:14).

If you know Jesus Christ as Saviour, you can expect victory because "greater is he that is in you, than he that is in the world" (I John 4:4). The Holy Spirit is within the believer, and the Devil is in the world. But how wonderful it is to realize that the indwelling Holy Spirit gives us victory over the flesh and the Devil as we respond to His leading and enablement.

Strategy of the Old Nature

It is important that the believer know the strategy of the old nature. The old nature, or flesh, is deceptive, because Satan works through it to defeat the believer. Satan is very wise, and he knows how to work through the desires of the flesh to tantalize and tempt the Christian.

On one occasion Jesus told His disciples, "Watch and pray, that ye enter not into temptation: the spirit indeed is willing, but the flesh is weak" (Matt. 26:41).

There is an excellent analogy between the way the flesh operates and the way Amalek worked as he attacked Israel. Later, in Deuteronomy, Moses told the Israelites, "Remember what Amalek did unto thee by the way, when ye were come forth out of Egypt; how he met thee by the way, and smote the hindmost of thee, even all that were feeble behind thee, when thou wast faint and weary; and he feared not God" (Deut. 25:17,18).

Notice the way Amalek attacked—he attacked from behind when the people were at their weakest. Amalek's method of attacking is also mentioned in I Samuel 15:2: "Thus saith the Lord of hosts, I remember that which Amalek did to Israel, how he laid wait for him in the way, when he came up from Egypt."

Satan works through the flesh to attack the believer in the same way. He sneaks up on the believer and attacks when he is at his weakest point. This is why the Bible says, "Be sober, be vigilant; because your adversary the devil, as a roaring lion, walketh about, seeking whom he may devour: whom resist stedfast in the faith" (I Pet. 5:8,9). These words of warning should alert believers to the deceitfulness of Satan.

But even though we grow weary and occasionally drop our guard, the Bible says, "Hast thou not known? Hast thou not heard, that the everlasting God, the Lord, the Creator of the ends of the earth, fainteth not, neither is weary? There is no searching of his understanding. He giveth power to the faint; and to them that have no might he increaseth strength. Even the youths shall faint and be weary, and the young men shall utterly fall: but they that wait upon the Lord shall renew their strength; they shall mount up with wings as eagles; they shall run, and not be weary; and they shall walk, and not faint" (Isa. 40:28-31). This is the victory God promises each believer. How wonderful it is to realize that God even now gives complete victory over Satan (Heb. 2:14) and will eventually completely destroy Satan and all of his forces.

Final Victory

After Joshua had defeated Amalek and his people by means of Moses' intercessory prayer on the hilltop, the Lord said to Moses, "Write this for a memorial in a book, and rehearse it in the ears of Joshua: for I will utterly put out the remembrance of Amalek from under heaven" (Ex. 17:14). Although Amalek would eventually be blotted out, Israel had to contend with him and his descendants for many, many years. So, too, even though the believer will eventually be delivered from the presence of sin, he must contend with the sin nature as long as he lives in his body of flesh.

Paul referred to his expectation of being delivered from the presence of sin when he said, "We ourselves groan within ourselves, waiting for the adoption, to wit, the redemption of our body" (Rom. 8:23). Philippians 3:21 says that Jesus Christ "shall change our vile body, that it may be fashioned like unto his glorious body, according to the working whereby he is able even to subdue all things unto himself." When our body experiences this change, we will be delivered from the presence of sin.

That every believer will someday receive a glorified body is also mentioned in I Corinthians 15:51-58. Verses 51 and 52 say, "Behold, I shew you a mystery; We shall not all sleep, but we shall all be changed, in a moment, in the twinkling of an eye, at the last trump: for the trumpet shall sound, and the dead shall be raised incorruptible, and we shall be changed." This refers to the time when Jesus Christ will appear in the air and catch away believers from the earth. Believers who have already died by that time will be raised first, then living believers will be caught up to meet the Lord (I Thess. 4:16,17).

Considering this time of victory, the Apostle Paul said, "O death, where is thy sting? O grave, where is thy victory?" (I Cor. 15:55). Because of the blessed hope of the complete triumph over sin, Paul said, "Therefore, my beloved brethren, be ye stedfast, unmoveable, always abounding in the work of the Lord, forasmuch as ye know that your labour is not in vain in the Lord" (v. 58). So remember, we can have victory over sin's dominion now, but we also have the glorious hope of deliverance from its presence at His coming. Can you say hallelujah because of this?

After God instructed Moses to write a memorial in a book concerning Amalek, Moses built an altar and called it "Jehovah-nissi" (Ex. 17:15). This reveals the confident assurance Moses had of God's ultimate victory over Amalek and his people. The name Moses gave the altar literally means "the Lord our banner." Moses was standing firm in the might and power of God over Amalek.

The New Testament tells believers, "Be strong in the Lord, and in the power of his might" (Eph. 6:10). Just like Moses, we are to realize that victory is certain because God is all powerful. Even now we can rejoice and praise God for the ultimate victory over the flesh which will occur when we receive glorified bodies (Phil. 3:20,21).

But as long as we are in this life, we need to be reminded of the tragedy of sparing the flesh. We learn this lesson from the way Saul spared Amalek, as recorded in I Samuel 15. God had told Saul to completely destroy all of the Amalekites and their livestock because of the way they had treated Israel, "but Saul and the people spared Agag, and the best of the sheep, and of the oxen, and of the fatlings, and the lambs, and all that was good, and would not utterly destroy them: but every thing that was vile and refuse, that they destroyed utterly" (v. 9).

When Saul was confronted by Samuel for his disobedience, Saul tried to blame the people. Saul said, "But the people took of the spoil, sheep and oxen, the chief of the things which should have been utterly destroyed, to sacrifice unto the Lord thy God in Gilgal" (v. 21). Think of it! Saul was trying to cover up his disobedience by claiming that his motive was the worship of God. However, Samuel clearly made known to Saul God's attitude about such disobedience: "Hath the Lord as great delight in burnt-offerings and sacrifices, as in obeying the voice of the Lord? Behold, to obey is better than sacrifice, and to hearken than the fat of rams" (v. 22).

Because of Saul's incomplete obedience, the Amalekites troubled him to his dying day. In fact, an Amalekite had a part in Saul's death.

Let us not spare the flesh and the works of the flesh, but rather by the Holy Spirit let us put to death everything that has to do with the old nature. This is the only way of victory for the child of God.

Chapter 14

Delegating Responsibility

God always works through people. When He has a job to do, He calls a person to do it. That is exactly what He did in leading the nation of Israel. For the gigantic task of leading Israel from Egypt to Canaan, God called Moses at the burning bush (Ex. 3).

Advice From Jethro

God prepared and strengthened Moses for this enormous responsibility—God always gives a person the ability he needs to perform the task He calls that individual to do. As Moses led the Israelites through the wilderness, however, he became burdened with the heavy responsibility of leadership. When Moses' father-in-law came to visit him in the wilderness, he observed that Moses spent a whole day deciding small and great matters for the people. "Moses sat to judge the people: and the people stood by Moses from the morning unto the evening" (18:13). When he saw this, Moses' father-in-law asked him why he was doing all of this by himself and why the people were standing from morning until evening (v. 14). Moses explained that they were bringing their problems to him so he could make decisions for them and teach the people God's laws (v. 16).

Moses' father-in-law said to him, "The thing that thou doest is not good. Thou wilt surely wear away, both thou, and this people that is with thee: for this thing is too heavy for thee; thou art not able to perform it thyself alone" (vv. 17,18).

Moses' father-in-law then explained what he thought was a much better method of administration: "I will give thee counsel, and God shall be with thee: Be thou for the people to God-ward, that thou mayest bring the causes unto God: and thou shalt teach them ordinances and laws, and shalt shew them the way wherein they must walk, and the work that they must do" (vv. 19,20). The suggestions of Jethro retained for Moses the position of representing God to the people and of teaching the people God's laws and ordinances.

But Jethro had still other suggestions concerning how Moses could relieve himself of the heavy responsibility: "Moreover thou shalt provide out of all the people able men, such as fear God, men of truth, hating covetousness; and place such over them, to be rulers of thousands, and rulers of hundreds, rulers of fifties, and rulers of tens: and let them judge the people at all seasons: and it shall be, that every great matter they shall bring unto thee, but every small matter they shall judge: so shall it be easier for thyself, and they shall bear the burden with thee" (vv. 21,22). Thus, Jethro suggested that Moses delegate responsibility to qualified men who feared God.

Jethro continued, "If thou shalt do this thing, and God command thee so, then thou shalt be able to endure, and all this people shall also go to their place in peace" (v. 23). So the suggestions of Jethro were intended to relieve the heavy burden that was on Moses personally and, at the same time, to make sure that the people had someone to help them make wise, godly decisions.

Some think that the suggestions of Jethro were of the flesh. However, Jethro emphasized that Moses should determine the Lord's will before accepting his suggestions. Jethro said, "I will give thee counsel, and God shall be with thee" (v. 19); "If thou shalt do this thing, and God command thee so" (v. 23). So Jethro was well aware that Moses should not adopt his suggestions unless God directed him to do so. Thus, the advice of Jethro seems to have been given in the right spirit; he was used of God to wisely advise Moses.

Do you wonder what Moses thought when Jethro suggested that he give up some of his responsibility? Most of us have the tendency to hold on to responsibility rather than to delegate it to others. One of the lessons I had to learn in the Back to the Bible ministry was the need to delegate responsibility as the ministry grew beyond what I could do personally. This was not an easy lesson to learn. Over the years God had to use various methods and individuals to help me face this need. I will never forget the day when this lesson was driven home to me in an especially pointed way. Our organization was small at the time, with only eight or ten employees. The work responsibility was very heavy on me personally. At that time a certain person told me, "Mr. Epp, there's just one problem with you; you can't let go of anything."

Inwardly, I reacted against that remark, but as I went to the Lord concerning it, He made clear to me that this person was speaking the truth. God had used this young person to reveal something about myself that I desperately needed to see.

Advice can be misleading, however. So it is the responsibility of every person receiving advice to go to the Lord for guidance and direction. This was Moses' responsibility, and it is what Jethro expected him to do.

Principles of Leadership

As I have studied the Word of God concerning leadership, I have come to certain conclusions about spiritual principles of good leadership. These principles can be applied not only by leaders of organizations but by Sunday school teachers or by anyone with responsibility.

First, God uses people to do His work. When He has a job to do, He calls an individual to do it. We have seen this in our study of Moses, and I am sure you have also seen it in your own experience and observation. Remember, however, that it took Moses a long time to become prepared for his task, and it sometimes takes leaders today a long time to be prepared for their tasks.

Second, when the task becomes too much for the one person God originally called, He calls others to work with the first individual. This principle is illustrated over and over again in the Word of God.

Third, God holds the first individual responsible for the work done by the other individuals. This principle applies

especially to the spiritual aspects of the work. This principle
was particularly evident in Moses' leadership. Even though
responsibility and authority could be delegated to others, he
was still directly responsible before God. Jethro said to him,
"Be thou for the people to God-ward, that thou mayest bring
the causes unto God" (Ex. 18:19). Another translation
renders this verse: "You be the people's representative before
God, and you bring the disputes to God" (NASB). Literally,
this portion reads: "You be for the people in front of God."

Even though Moses could delegate much of his
responsibility and authority, he could not delegate this
primary responsibility of spiritual leadership.

Moses accepted Jethro's advice; he "hearkened to the
voice of his father in law, and did all that he had said. And
Moses chose able men out of all Israel, and made them heads
over the people, rulers of thousands, rulers of hundreds,
rulers of fifties, and rulers of tens. And they judged the
people at all seasons: the hard causes they brought unto
Moses, but every small matter they judged themselves"
(vv. 24-26).

Examples of Delegation

In a parallel passage where Moses revealed to God his
weariness and inability to take care of all of the
responsibilities, he was admonished to delegate responsibility
to 70 men (Num. 11). Verse 25 says, "The Lord came down
in a cloud, and spake unto him, and took of the spirit that
was upon him, and gave it unto the seventy elders: and it
came to pass, that, when the spirit rested upon them, they
prophesied, and did not cease." Some say that there was no
more power than before, just more machinery. But this
viewpoint does not seem to be realistic or even scriptural.

Jesus Himself chose 12 men, and later He chose others,
like Paul, to carry on His work. And even Paul was given the
right to choose others to assist him.

So I cannot agree with those who think that there was a
diminishing of the Spirit that rested on Moses, for it is very
difficult to think of the Spirit's being subdivided. You cannot
draw the Spirit from one man and divide Him among others
as you draw water and divide it among several containers. So

the indication is that Numbers 11:25 refers to taking the same Spirit which was on Moses, and putting Him on the 70 others. Just as a flame of fire increases as it reaches out and engulfs more objects, so the Holy Spirit is made more effective by His extension to other lives.

In the Exodus account Moses accepted the advice of his father-in-law, appointed qualified men for the responsibility, and became an even greater mediator between God and the people. This is evident as we study the rest of Moses' life. Whenever the people murmured or whenever God's judgment fell on the people, Moses interceded mightily. As the mediator, Moses received the Law and communicated it to the people. In his responsibility of spiritual leadership, the Book of Deuteronomy records how he rehearsed for the younger generation the faithfulness of God to their fathers in the wilderness. Moses wanted to make sure that they did not forget God's faithfulness when they entered the Promised Land.

The New Testament also reveals principles for spiritual leadership. When the physical needs of some were neglected, the apostles realized they could not take on this kind of responsibility and still remain faithful to prayer and the study of the Word. So the apostles instructed, "It is not reason [desirable] that we should leave the word of God, and serve tables. Wherefore, brethren, look ye out among you seven men of honest report, full of the Holy Ghost and wisdom, whom we may appoint over this business. But we will give ourselves continually to prayer, and to the ministry of the word" (Acts 6:2-4). No one can do everything, so those who have the responsibility of prayer and the ministry of the Word must delegate the responsibility of other important matters to qualified, Spirit-filled people.

The following is a good motto: "If you cannot learn to delegate, your ministry will never become larger than that which you are able to dominate."

God knows what work He wants accomplished, and He gives individuals responsibilities in order to accomplish that work. The only way that God's work can be done effectively is for individual believers to know what God wants them to do.

Holy Spirit's Sovereignty

In studying the Scriptures concerning God's work, we learn that the primary work being done today has to do with the building of the Church. Jesus Christ said, "I will build my church; and the gates of hell shall not prevail against it" (Matt. 16:18). However, the Holy Spirit has been delegated the responsibility of directing the work of building the Church. Before the Lord Jesus ascended to heaven, He told the disciples that He would send the Holy Spirit (John 14:16; 16:7). The Holy Spirit has been given absolute sovereignty in choosing the individuals and distributing gifts to accomplish God's work.

First Corinthians 12 tells of the spiritual gifts given by the Holy Spirit to believers so that the Body of Christ may fulfill its purpose on earth. Verse 7 indicates that every believer has a spiritual gift: "The manifestation of the Spirit is given to every man to profit withal." Verse 11 reveals that these gifts are given, not as an individual might desire, but as the Holy Spirit desires: "All these worketh that one and the selfsame Spirit, dividing to every man severally as he will." Each believer has a particular work to perform within the Body of Christ. Verse 18 says, "But now hath God set the members every one of them in the body, as it hath pleased him." So we are not to serve our own desires but to discover what God wants us to do. Then we are to use our spiritual gift to benefit the Body of Christ.

Today, there is a great deal of emphasis on methods. When people are concerned about increasing the effectiveness of a given work, they usually look for better methods. However, God uses people. Instead of seeking better methods, He wants individuals who will do His will. The Lord Jesus Christ said, "Ye have not chosen me, but I have chosen you, and ordained you, that ye should go and bring forth fruit" (John 15:16).

Throughout the Scriptures we read of those who were chosen of God to accomplish His purpose. In the Old Testament we learn that He chose such men as Abraham, Isaac and Jacob to perform His distinctive purposes. In the New Testament men like the Apostle Paul were distinctly chosen of God to take the gospel to the Gentiles. But

whoever the individual is, the Holy Spirit chooses him and
equips him with the spiritual gift necessary to accomplish
God's purpose. The gift the individual possesses is the
sovereign choice of the Holy Spirit rather than a selection of
the individual himself. Thus, we need to see that the Holy
Spirit is absolutely sovereign in His administrative work of
choosing men, giving gifts and placing individuals where He
desires.

Chapter 15

The Giving of the Law

Exodus 19 and 20 record an event that was a great turning point in the life of Israel as well as all mankind. These chapters record the giving of the Law by God through Moses to the nation of Israel.

Time Elements

Exodus 19:1,2 says, "In the third month, when the children of Israel were gone forth out of the land of Egypt, the same day came they into the wilderness of Sinai. For they were departed from Rephidim, and were come to the desert of Sinai, and had pitched in the wilderness; and there Israel camped before the mount."

God fulfilled His promise to Moses. When God had called Moses at the burning bush in the wilderness of Sinai, He said, "I will be with thee; and this shall be a token unto thee, that I have sent thee: When thou hast brought forth the people out of Egypt, ye shall serve God upon this mountain" (3:12). Moses and the Israelites were now at Mount Sinai, thus fulfilling God's promise to him.

Notice three specific time elements mentioned in the Bible concerning Israel at Mount Sinai. Exodus 19:1 says, "In the third month, when the children of Israel were gone forth out of the land of Egypt, the same day came they into the wilderness of Sinai." This was the beginning of the third month; it had taken them two months to reach this spot from the time they left Egypt.

Numbers 1:1 says, "The Lord spake unto Moses in the wilderness of Sinai, in the tabernacle of the congregation, on

151

the first day of the second month, in the second year after they were come out of the land of Egypt." At this time the Lord told Moses to number the people in preparation for leaving Mount Sinai. By comparing the time elements, we find that the Israelites were at Mount Sinai 11 months. During that time God gave the Law, and they built the tabernacle according to His instructions.

But after leaving Mount Sinai and coming to Kadesh-barnea, the people refused to enter the land. They failed God completely. Thus, they wandered in the wilderness for another 38 years. At the end of that time they again found themselves at Mount Sinai with God's giving them instructions to enter the land. "It came to pass in the fortieth year, in the eleventh month, on the first day of the month, that Moses spake unto the children of Israel, according unto all that the Lord had given him in commandment unto them . . . saying, The Lord our God spake unto us in Horeb, saying, Ye have dwelt long enough in this mount: turn you, and take your journey, and go to the mount of the Amorites, and unto all the places nigh thereunto, in the plain, in the hills, and in the vale, and in the south, and by the sea side, to the land of the Canaanites, and unto Lebanon, unto the great river, the river Euphrates" (Deut. 1:3,5-7). These references in Exodus, Numbers and Deuteronomy make it clear that Mount Sinai figured prominently in the life of Israel during the 40 years it took them to go from Egypt to Canaan.

At Mount Sinai the covenant by which God would deal with them for about the next 1500 years was given. In other words, this covenant remained in effect until the Lord Jesus Christ was crucified at Calvary, thus changing the order of God's dealings with mankind.

At Sinai, at the beginning of the third month after the Israelites had left Egypt, God gave the people a wondrous manifestation of Himself as He gave them a new covenant. Think of God's true revelation in comparison with some of the revelations which have been claimed by various religious groups. Claims are often made by those who have nothing tangible to prove their claims, but God made sure that the Israelites knew absolutely that His revelation was true. Those who claim to have found stones and yet have no stones to offer for inspection are highly suspect. Others base their so-called revelation on dreams or visions. But God erased all questions as to the truth of His revelation to Israel.

Contrasting Covenants

Note the contrast between the covenant God made with Abraham and the covenant He made with Israel through Moses. The covenant with Abraham was an unconditional covenant—God promised to fulfill it regardless of the circumstances. It was based on God's eternal purpose and did not depend on man's behavior at all.

Genesis 12:1-3 records the Abrahamic covenant: "Now the Lord had said unto Abram, Get thee out of thy country, and from thy kindred, and from thy father's house, unto a land that I will shew thee: and I will make of thee a great nation, and I will bless thee, and make thy name great; and thou shalt be a blessing: and I will bless them that bless thee, and curse him that curseth thee: and in thee shall all families of the earth be blessed."

The Abrahamic covenant contained seven promises but not one condition. This covenant was confirmed later in Genesis 17:6-8: "I will make thee exceeding fruitful, and I will make nations of thee, and kings shall come out of thee. And I will establish my covenant between me and thee and thy seed after thee in their generations for an everlasting covenant, to be a God unto thee, and to thy seed after thee. And I will give unto thee, and to thy seed after thee, the land wherein thou art a stranger, all the land of Canaan, for an everlasting possession; and I will be their God." The covenant was not only confirmed but was also made everlasting.

God's covenant with Abraham was an unconditional one, but His covenant with Israel through Moses was a conditional one. God promised great benefits if the Israelites met the conditions. Personal and temporal blessings depended entirely on their behavior, based on the covenant of the Law. However, this Mosaic covenant in no way altered the plan and purpose of God as revealed in the Abrahamic covenant. The Abrahamic covenant was unconditional and will remain unchanged until it is completely fulfilled after the Second Coming of Christ. The Mosaic covenant was conditional and was fulfilled by Christ at His first coming.

When Jesus Christ was on earth, He said, "Think not that I am come to destroy the law, or the prophets: I am not come to destroy, but to fulfil. For verily I say unto you, Till heaven and earth pass, one jot or one tittle shall in no wise pass from the law, till all be fulfilled" (Matt. 5:17,18). Galatians 3:19 reveals how long the Mosaic covenant would be in force: "Wherefore then serveth the law? It was added because of transgressions, till the seed should come to whom the promise was made; and it was ordained by angels in the hand of a mediator." Note that "it was added because of transgressions, till the seed should come to whom the promise was made." This was fulfilled at the first coming of Christ.

At Sinai God's dealings with the Israelites changed completely. Up until this time, God had led the people from Egypt to Sinai on the basis of His unconditional covenant with Abraham. At Sinai God told the people, "Ye have seen what I did unto the Egyptians, and how I bare you on eagles' wings, and brought you unto myself" (Ex. 19:4).

As God led the people on the basis of the Abrahamic covenant during the first two months after they left Egypt, He did not in any way judge them because of their murmurings. They had witnessed the plagues in Egypt, they had seen God's display of power at the Red Sea, they had experienced the guidance of the pillar of cloud and the pillar of fire, they had witnessed God's grace in providing manna and water, and they had won victory over Amalek and his people. Certainly God had borne them on eagles' wings, for He had taken care of all their needs even though they were grumbling and complaining much of the time. Even though the people were unfaithful, God was faithful to His promises; He never denies Himself (II Tim. 2:13). God was faithful to the promises He made to Abraham and to his seed.

That God was being faithful to His promise to Abraham is clear from what the Bible says concerning His attitude toward Israel while they were still in Egypt. Exodus 2:24 says, "God heard their groaning, and God remembered his covenant with Abraham, with Isaac, and with Jacob." In response to this covenant, God intervened to deliver the Israelites from Egypt—not because of any actions of the Israelites but because He was faithful to His unconditional covenant with Abraham. Psalm 105 tells of the many things God did for Israel in delivering them from Egypt, and the basis of all of these provisions is stated in verse 42: "For he remembered his holy promise, and Abraham his servant."

But at Sinai God began to deal with the Israelites on a different basis. The conditions involved in God's dealings with the Israelites are seen in Exodus 19:5,6: "Now therefore, if ye will obey my voice indeed, and keep my covenant, then ye shall be a peculiar treasure unto me above all people: for all the earth is mine: and ye shall be unto me a kingdom of priests, and an holy nation." This is what God instructed Moses to communicate to the Israelites. The conditions of the covenant are expressed in the words, "if ye will obey my voice indeed, and keep my covenant" (v. 5).

This reference was not to the Abrahamic covenant because there were no conditions attached to it. In fact, on the basis of the Abrahamic covenant God is fulfilling and will continue to fulfill His sovereign plan to eventually regather the nation of Israel in Palestine and fully establish them as a nation that will inherit the land. But at Sinai God added another covenant between Himself and Israel which involved conditions. Israel was required to meet the conditions if they were to expect the blessings connected with that covenant.

Unanimous Acceptance

At Sinai Israel overwhelmingly accepted God's proposal to enter into the legal covenant. The people were in unanimous agreement and said, "All that the Lord hath spoken we will do" (v. 8). After God had revealed His high standards to the Israelites through the Law, they said again, "All that the Lord hath said will we do, and be obedient" (24:7). This covenant was then confirmed and ratified by blood.

Later, when the Israelites entered Canaan, they were under the Mosaic covenant. But from Mount Sinai onward, because the people were bound by a conditional covenant, God dealt with them by chastening them whenever they failed, as they did at Kadesh-barnea. Also, after the people had entered the land of Canaan, God dealt with them there on the basis of the Mosaic covenant. He allowed persecution, and later He even permitted the people to be expelled from the land for disobedience.

Grace and Good Works

Just as there were two covenants for Israel, there are two different aspects of God's relationship with the believer. Concerning salvation, God's relationship with the believer is one entirely of grace. An unregenerate person can do absolutely nothing that merits standing before God. Salvation is totally of grace. Ephesians 2:8,9 says, "For by grace are ye saved through faith; and that not of yourselves: it is the gift of God: not of works, lest any man should boast." But one should not stop reading at verse 9, because verse 10 gives the second aspect of God's relationship with a believer. This aspect involves the works produced after salvation. Verse 10 says, "For we are his workmanship, created in Christ Jesus unto good works, which God hath before ordained that we should walk in them."

Although a person receives salvation entirely by grace through faith in Jesus Christ, it is God's purpose that he produce good works after salvation, which He rewards accordingly.

These two aspects of God's relationship to the believer are also seen in Romans 5. Salvation by grace through faith is seen in verses 8 and 9: "But God commendeth his love toward us, in that, while we were yet sinners, Christ died for us. Much more then, being now justified by his blood, we shall be saved from wrath through him." We did not deserve God's love—we were still sinners when He died for us.

The aspects of grace extended for salvation and the intention of God that a believer's life produce good works is seen in verse 10: "For if, when we were enemies, we were reconciled to God by the death of his Son, much more, being reconciled, we shall be saved by his life." Concerning salvation, we can do nothing except believe in what Jesus Christ has done for us. But after receiving Christ as Saviour, we are to produce good works by allowing Christ to live in us.

The two aspects of grace for salvation and the producing of works after salvation are also seen in I Corinthians 3. Salvation is seen in the foundation referred to in verse 11:

"For other foundation can no man lay than that is laid, which is Jesus Christ." The producing of works after salvation and the rewarding of such works are emphasized in verses 12-15: "Now if any man build upon this foundation gold, silver, precious stones, wood, hay, stubble; every man's work shall be made manifest: for the day shall declare it, because it shall be revealed by fire; and the fire shall try every man's work of what sort it is. If any man's work shall be burned, he shall suffer loss: but he himself shall be saved; yet so as by fire."

Why is such a person saved even though he produces no good work to be rewarded? It is because a person's salvation does not depend on good works but on the grace of God. Any person who realizes his need and trusts Jesus Christ as personal Saviour is a child of God, regardless of the amount of good works he produces later. However, where there are no good works, God chastens the believer so that he will produce those things which honor Him.

Philippians 2 tells how good works are to be produced in the life of a believer. Verses 12,13 say, "Wherefore, my beloved, as ye have always obeyed, not as in my presence only, but now much more in my absence, work out your own salvation with fear and trembling. For it is God which worketh in you both to will and to do of his good pleasure." Notice that this passage does not say an individual is to work for his salvation, but he is to work out his salvation. Before a person can work out his salvation, he must already have salvation. The one who has trusted Jesus Christ as personal Saviour has salvation; therefore, he has the Lord Jesus Christ living within him. The believer produces good works as he allows the Lord Jesus Christ to work out His life through him.

Transition Periods

It is commonly taught that a new dispensation began at Mount Sinai. However, the distinctiveness of Israel as a nation actually began on the Passover night in Egypt. In most of the dispensations there is an overlapping from one to the other—a transition period. This is true in this case also. Although the Law was given to the Israelites at Mount Sinai, the people had actually become a nation two months earlier in Egypt. Up until that time they had been a multitude of disorganized slaves, but they became an organized nation led by God Himself through His servant Moses.

On the Passover night for the first time the people were called an "assembly" (Ex. 12:6), and their calendar was dated from that time forward by divine order (v. 2).

Before the Law was actually given on Mount Sinai, the people were not without a covenant; they still had the unconditional covenant made with Abraham. But, as recorded in Exodus 19 and 20, the Mosaic covenant came into operation and specifically concerned Israel. So there was a transition period of about two months from the time they became a nation in Egypt until they actually received the Law at Mount Sinai.

The Dispensation of Grace, the present dispensation, was also marked by a transition period. When Jesus Christ died on the cross, He made it possible for every person to have immediate access to God. At His crucifixion, the veil of the temple was torn from top to bottom, and the Book of Hebrews says, "Having therefore, brethren, boldness to enter into the holiest by the blood of Jesus, by a new and living way, which he hath consecrated for us, through the veil, that is to say, his flesh" (10:19,20). But even though Jesus Christ ended the Dispensation of the Law when He died on the cross, it was not until 50 days later, on the Day of Pentecost, that the Holy Spirit came to indwell every believer, thereby marking the official opening of the new dispensation. So there was a transition period of at least 50 days between those two dispensations.

The Mediator and the Message

At Mount Sinai Moses was established by God as the mediator of a new revelation from Him. Because God is holy, He could not enter into direct communication with the sinful nation of Israel, but He worked through a mediator. Moses was God's special vessel whom He used for this occasion. Therefore, Moses needed to receive special credentials to establish confidence with the people that he was indeed God's spokesman to them.

Many false religions have arisen with claims about dreams revealed to certain people or concerning tablets and other objects that have been found. Yet, when these claims are investigated, no hard evidence can be found to indicate that God revealed Himself in such a way to them.

God saw to it that the Israelites would know for sure that what He was revealing to them through Moses was really of Him. Thus, God spoke audibly with Moses, and the people heard God speaking on the mountain. This established Moses' credentials, proving that he was indeed the mediator between God and the people. God said to Moses, "I come unto thee in a thick cloud, that the people may hear when I speak with thee, and believe thee for ever" (Ex. 19:9).

We see from the Bible that God provided credentials concerning Himself through Jesus Christ. John 1:14 says of Christ, "The Word was made flesh, and dwelt among us, (and we beheld his glory, the glory as of the only begotten of the Father,) full of grace and truth." God saw to it that Jesus Christ was seen in person. What tremendous credentials for God Himself. God became flesh in the Person of Jesus Christ. Thus, Jesus was able to say, "He that hath seen me hath seen the Father" (14:9).

As God gave the Law to Israel, He spoke audibly from the mountaintop. The Bible says, "So Moses went down unto the people, and spake unto them" (Ex. 19:25). But notice that the following verse says, "And God spake all these words" (20:1). The audible voice of God was proof that Moses was the leader of Israel and that the Law had come directly from God.

Later, when Moses reviewed the history of Israel for the people, he said, "Ye came near and stood under the mountain; and the mountain burned with fire unto the midst of heaven, with darkness, clouds, and thick darkness. And the Lord spake unto you out of the midst of the fire: ye heard the voice of the words, but saw no similitude; only ye heard a voice. And he declared unto you his covenant, which he commanded you to perform, even ten commandments; and he wrote them upon two tables of stone" (Deut. 4:11-13).

Moses also told the people, "The Lord our God made a covenant with us in Horeb. . . . The Lord talked with you face to face in the mount out of the midst of the fire"

(5:2,4). But what was the peoples' reaction when they heard the voice of God at Mount Sinai? Exodus 20:18 says, "And all the people saw the thunderings, and the lightnings, and the noise of the trumpet, and the mountain smoking: and when the people saw it, they removed, and stood afar off." These people were frightened because of all that was taking place. They said to Moses, "Speak thou with us, and we will hear: but let not God speak with us, lest we die" (v. 19).

Moses told the people, "Fear not: for God is come to prove you, and that his fear may be before your faces, that ye sin not" (v. 20). As the people stood a long way off, Moses "drew near unto the thick darkness where God was" (v. 21).

The Lord said to Moses, "Thus thou shalt say unto the children of Israel, Ye have seen that I have talked with you from heaven" (v. 22). Notice that the people heard God speak from heaven. Their reaction was one of fear, and they begged Moses to speak with them instead of God. Thus, Moses was established before the people as the official mediator between God and them. This is what God desired, because He eventually spoke all of the Law through Moses. However, God wanted the people to realize that the Law was not some concoction of Moses himself, so He gave credentials to establish Moses and the message before their eyes. As a result, the people never doubted the true origin of the Law.

The purpose of God in all of this was alluded to earlier: "The Lord said unto Moses, Lo, I come unto thee in a thick cloud, that the people may hear when I speak with thee, and believe thee for ever" (19:9). God wanted the people to hear Him speaking audibly so they would not doubt the authority of Moses as the mediator or the validity of the message.

A Way to Meet God

By giving the Law, God did not cease to deal with Israel on the basis of grace and mercy, because He did provide a way through which Israel could always meet Him—the ceremonial law. So whereas God provided the Ten Commandments, which the people could not keep—although they said that they would keep them—God also provided the ceremonial law by which they could approach Him. The people were intensely aware of their inability to stand in the presence of God; thus, they "stood afar off" (Ex. 20:21). But in His mercy God provided an altar on which the Israelites could offer sacrifices so that they would be able to enter His presence (vv. 24-26).

Concerning the Law, the Scofield Reference Bible notes, "There is a threefold giving of the law. First, orally, in Ex. 20. 1-17. This was pure law, with no provision of priesthood and sacrifice for failure, and was accompanied by the 'judgments' (Ex. 21. 1-23. 13) relating to the relations of Hebrew with Hebrew; to which were added (Ex. 23. 14-19) directions for keeping three annual feasts, and (Ex. 23. 20-33) instructions for the conquest of Canaan. These *words* Moses communicated to the people (Ex. 24. 3-8). Immediately, in the persons of their elders, they were admitted to the fellowship of God (Ex. 24. 9-11). Second, Moses was then called up to receive the *tables* of stone (Ex. 24. 12-18). The story then divides. Moses, in the mount, receives the gracious instructions concerning the tabernacle, priesthood, and sacrifice (Ex. 25.-31.). Meantime (Ex. 32.), the people, led by Aaron, break the first commandment. Moses, returning, breaks the tables 'written with the finger of God' (Ex. 31. 18; 32. 16-19). Third, the *second* tables were made by Moses, and the law again written by the hand of Jehovah (Ex. 34. 1,28,29; Deut. 10. 4)" (p. 95).

Chapter 16

God Meets His People

In considering all that took place on Mount Sinai, we need to retrace some of the events and highlight some of the important details.

Requirements for Meeting God

As the people were being prepared to meet Him, God said to Moses, "Go unto the people, and sanctify them to day and to morrow, and let them wash their clothes, and be ready against the third day: for the third day the Lord will come down in the sight of all the people upon mount Sinai" (Ex. 19:10,11).

In addition to going through the process of cleansing before they could meet God, the people also had definite bounds set for them. God told Moses, "Thou shalt set bounds unto the people round about, saying, Take heed to yourselves, that ye go not up into the mount, or touch the border of it: whosoever toucheth the mount shall be surely put to death: there shall not an hand touch it, but he shall surely be stoned, or shot through; whether it be beast or man, it shall not live: when the trumpet soundeth long, they shall come up to the mount" (vv. 12,13).

All of this emphasized the contrast between the holiness of God and the sinfulness of man. God was unable to allow sinful men to come directly into His presence without a process of cleansing and the setting of definite limitations. But in the meeting He had with the people, God gave them the way of access to Himself.

Just as God revealed the way through which the Israelites could approach Him, so He has revealed a way by which we can approach Him. When Jesus Christ died on the cross in our place, this way was opened. Hebrews 10:19,20 says, "Having therefore, brethren, boldness to enter into the holiest by the blood of Jesus, by a new and living way, which he hath consecrated for us, through the veil, that is to say, his flesh." Through what Jesus Christ accomplished in His physical body on the cross, the way of access to God has been opened to all believers. Previously, the veil of the temple had kept the people away from the presence of God, but through His death Jesus Christ made access available to all.

In the case of the Israelites, death would come to anyone who even touched the mountain on which God revealed Himself. Such instructions emphasized the holiness of God to the people. Then they were really awed on the third day, for "there were thunders and lightnings, and a thick cloud upon the mount, and the voice of the trumpet exceeding loud; so that all the people that was in the camp trembled. And Moses brought forth the people out of the camp to meet with God; and they stood at the nether part of the mount. And mount Sinai was altogether on a smoke, because the Lord descended upon it in fire: and the smoke thereof ascended as the smoke of a furnace, and the whole mount quaked greatly. And when the voice of the trumpet sounded long, and waxed louder and louder, Moses spake, and God answered him by a voice" (Ex. 19:16-19).

The people were not to approach God until He revealed the way, and then they had to come in precisely that way. The people trembled, and it is certainly easy to understand why they were afraid of God, who is absolutely holy and who was giving instructions to them through Moses.

But notice God's purpose in all of this. Moses told the people, "Fear not: for God is come to prove you, and that his fear may be before your faces, that ye sin not" (20:20). In the light of all that happened at Mount Sinai, it is strange that some people today think they can come to God in any way they want. The way into God's presence has been made possible through the shedding of the blood of the Lord Jesus Christ. But some deny the effectiveness of Christ's shed blood and yet think that they can come into the presence of

God. Were it not for the shed blood of the Lord Jesus Christ, we would all remain in sin, for Hebrews 9:22 says, "Almost all things are by the law purged with blood; and without shedding of blood is no remission [forgiveness]." That more people do not die at the hands of God because of their blasphemous ideas is only because of the longsuffering and mercy of God.

Those today who think they have access to God without coming on the basis of the shed blood of Christ are not really entering into the presence of God, or they would be struck dead, just as God threatened to destroy any Israelite who came in a way not prescribed. God is holy; He is absolutely righteous. He cannot be approached except through Jesus Christ, who is the Mediator between God and man (I Tim. 2:5). Jesus Christ became man in order that He might open the way to God for all mankind. God wanted to impress on the Israelites, and He wants to impress on us, that no one can come into His presence unless He comes by the prescribed way. Jesus said in John 14:6, "I am the way, the truth, and the life: no man cometh unto the Father, but by me."

The Majesty of God

God's appearance to the Israelites was accompanied by thunder and lightening, a reminder that His judgments are sure and that His voice is fearful. No wonder the Israelites trembled as they "saw the thunderings, and the lightnings, and the noise of the trumpet, and the mountain smoking" (Ex. 20:18).

In considering the glory, majesty and power of God and the trembling that is caused by His presence, notice what Psalm 114 says: "When Israel went out of Egypt, the house of Jacob from a people of strange language; Judah was his sanctuary, and Israel his dominion. The sea saw it, and fled: Jordan was driven back. The mountains skipped like rams, and the little hills like lambs. What ailed thee, O thou sea, that thou fleddest? Thou Jordan, that thou wast driven back? Ye mountains, that ye skipped like rams; and ye little hills, like lambs? Tremble, thou earth, at the presence of the Lord, at the presence of the God of Jacob; which turned the rock

into a standing water, the flint into a fountain of waters"
(vv. 1-8).

Fire is referred to in the Bible as a symbol of God. It is
awesome and causes people to fear because of its power to
consume. The Book of Hebrews warns, "See that ye refuse
not him that speaketh. For if they escaped not who refused
him that spake on earth, much more shall not we escape, if
we turn away from him that speaketh from heaven. . . . For
our God is a consuming fire" (12:25,29). No wonder
Hebrews 10:31 says, "It is a fearful thing to fall into the
hands of the living God."

It is my personal desire, and it should be the desire of
every Christian, to have a new and greater understanding of
the holiness of God. It is only because of His grace that any
of us are allowed to stand in His presence. No one is able to
stand before Him on the basis of his own merits. But how
terrible it would be to be totally beyond the benefits of
God's presence. That is why hell will be so horrible; none of
the benefits of His presence will be there. And remember, the
ones who go to hell are those who try to enter God's
presence on their own merits rather than on the merits of the
shed blood of the Lord Jesus Christ.

God instructed the Israelites not to touch the mountain
for the purpose of causing them to respect His holiness and
to tremble before Him. Note that believers are told to work
out their salvation "with fear and trembling" (Phil. 2:12).
Remember, this verse does not apply to gaining salvation,
because one must already have salvation before it can be
worked out through his life. This verse is instructing believers
how to live out the salvation which they have. Because of
salvation, Jesus Christ lives within the believer, and He wants
to express this salvation through the believer's life. The
believer should fear and tremble lest he miss God's will in his
daily walk.

The Israelites did not see the face of God or any likeness
of Him on Mount Sinai. But the audible voice they heard
provided evidence that He was there. So, too, we do not
worship a God who is seen by the naked eye. True, Christ
lived among men for a period of time, but He has gone to be
with the Father.

That we walk by faith and not by sight is evident from II Corinthians 5:16: "Wherefore henceforth know we no man after the flesh: yea, though we have known Christ after the flesh, yet now henceforth know we him no more [after the flesh]." And Jesus told the woman at the well, "The hour cometh, and now is, when the true worshippers shall worship the Father in spirit and in truth: for the Father seeketh such to worship him. God is a Spirit: and they that worship him must worship him in spirit and in truth" (John 4:23,24).

As God was about to ratify the Mosaic covenant, He presented Himself to the people and demonstrated His holiness so that they would be aware of the absolute righteousness of the One with whom they were making the covenant. God wanted the people to fear and tremble so that they would understand that they could never stand in His presence on the basis of their own merits.

God wanted the people to be impressed with His holiness to the extent that they would not sin. This is evident from what Moses told the people: "God is come to prove you, and that his fear may be before your faces, that ye sin not" (Ex. 20:20). Moses later reminded the Israelites, "Ye said, Behold, the Lord our God hath shewed us his glory and his greatness, and we have heard his voice out of the midst of the fire: we have seen this day that God doth talk with man, and he liveth" (Deut. 5:24).

A view of God's majesty such as Israel saw at Sinai is the crying need of our day. The eye of faith needs to see Him not only as a loving Father but also as "the high and lofty One that inhabiteth eternity, whose name is Holy" (Isa. 57:15). We also need to think of God as did Daniel, who spoke of Him as "the great and dreadful God" (Dan. 9:4).

Concerning this matter, I would encourage you to meditate on Isaiah 40. Notice especially verses 15, 17 and 18: "Behold, the nations are as a drop of a bucket, and are counted as the small dust of the balance: behold, he taketh up the isles as a very little thing. . . . All the nations before him are as nothing; and they are counted to him less than nothing, and vanity. To whom then will ye liken God? Or what likeness will ye compare unto him?"

This God of the Old Testament is also the God of the New Testament. And be sure to note that He is also our God.

Therefore, we should reverence Him, obey Him, worship Him and serve Him with fear and trembling.

God's Absolute Monarchy

From their time in Egypt until they arrived at Mount Sinai, God dealt with the Israelites in marvelous grace. He had borne with them in tender patience and had supplied their every need. On the shores of the Red Sea the people declared that Jehovah was indeed their God and that He should reign forever.

Exodus 15 records the great song they sang as they worshiped and praised God. The people declared, "The Lord is my strength and song, and he is become my salvation: he is my God, and I will prepare him an habitation; my father's God, and I will exalt him. The Lord is a man of war: the Lord is his name" (vv. 2,3). As they marveled at God's majesty, they said, "Who is like unto thee, O Lord, among the gods? Who is like thee, glorious in holiness, fearful in praises, doing wonders? . . . Thou in thy mercy hast led forth the people which thou hast redeemed: thou hast guided them in thy strength unto thy holy habitation" (vv. 11,13).

As they reached the climax of their song, they said, "The Lord shall reign for ever and ever" (v. 18). There was no doubt at that time concerning the devotion of the people to God; they had seen Him work in their behalf, and they rejoiced in His majesty and power.

However, the Israelites were to learn another basic lesson—that God was to reign as their absolute monarch. They had not yet seen that they were destined to be a kingdom and that God was to be their king.

The reality of God's government was at that time unrealistic to the Israelites. They didn't realize that God wanted them as His nation and that He wanted to be the absolute monarch over them. With their lips the Israelites acknowledged God as their ruler, yet primarily they saw only Moses as their leader, not God. They had not made Him their personal God.

So also, it is one thing for the believer today to exalt God in his soul and heart, but it is quite another thing for the believer to recognize God as the absolute monarch in his life.

Perhaps we can sing praises to the majesty of God when we are with a crowd of believers, and perhaps we can say amen when a great sermon is preached, but do we really recognize God as the absolute monarch in our lives? Are we looking to human leaders, or are we looking to *the* leader?

The Israelites needed to see God, not Moses, as their real leader, legislator, lawgiver and king. After all, Moses was only a mouthpiece for God, an intermediary to communicate God's decrees to the people.

Israel had reached the point where the people needed to be taught that God had righteous claims on them. They needed to see that God was a personal God to them. They needed to recognize that His throne had to be established over them in reality and that His authority had to be acknowledged personally. They needed to recognize that His will was supreme and that it must always regulate their lives. They needed to recognize themselves as a redeemed people whom God had bought for Himself. They were under the deepest possible obligation to fear, obey and serve God.

But remember that I Corinthians 10:11 says, "All these things happened unto them for ensamples: and they are written for our admonition, upon whom the ends of the world are come." We are to learn from the example of the Israelites. We, too, need to recognize that this God—the God of Abraham, Isaac, Jacob, Moses and Israel—is also our God.

While in divine love God provided the Law, the main purpose for His giving it was to maintain His authority. Israel had to see that they were under His government. God continued to reveal grace and mercy to the people—He prescribed in the ceremonial law how they could enter His presence. Through sacrifices the people were able to obtain forgiveness of sin.

Until the Law was given through Moses, God had worked with the Israelites on the basis of the Abrahamic covenant. Although the Abrahamic covenant still remained in force, God began to work with the people on the basis of their behavior. If they obeyed, He blessed; if they disobeyed, He withheld blessing and even permitted severe chastening. However, the national blessings involving a land, descendants and spiritual blessings still depended on the Abrahamic covenant (Gen. 12:1-3). Today, many Jews—descendants of

Abraham—are returning to the land. Although most are returning in unbelief, a national conversion will eventually take place (Rom. 11:26).

A reading of the account of God's revealing Himself to the people at Mount Sinai seems to reveal that the people evidenced a haughty attitude. They immediately responded, "All that the Lord hath spoken we will do" (Ex. 19:8). Yet, they had been guilty of grumbling and complaining against Moses (actually against God), and after making this promise, they were frequently guilty of the same thing. They were quick to say they would obey God, but they were slow to practice it. They were much like those referred to in the New Testament: "For if any be a hearer of the word, and not a doer, he is like unto a man beholding his natural face in a glass: for he beholdeth himself, and goeth his way, and straightway forgetteth what manner of man he was" (James 1:23,24).

May those of us who know Jesus Christ as Saviour not be guilty of the same thing. Let us be like those mentioned in verse 25: "But whoso looketh into the perfect law of liberty, and continueth therein, he being not a forgetful hearer, but a doer of the work, this man shall be blessed in his deed."

Chapter 17

The Law's Time and Purpose

Much confusion exists today concerning the time the
Law spanned and what its actual purpose was. Some say that
the Law was to be in effect from the time it was given until
the end of time. Others say the Law was binding only until
the time of Christ. Some say the purpose of the Law is to
provide salvation to those who keep it; others say no one can
be saved by keeping the Law. These are tremendously
important subjects, and the crucial question that needs
answering is, What does the Bible indicate about the Law's
time and purpose?

Galatians 3:19 is a key verse concerning this matter:
"Wherefore then serveth the law? It was added because of
transgressions, till the seed should come to whom the
promise was made; and it was ordained by angels in the hand
of a mediator." Notice three important elements in this
verse: the Law had a beginning—"it was added"; the Law had
a reason for being given—"because of transgressions"; the
Law was destined to have an end—"till the seed should
come."

The Law's Beginning

Let us now consider these three elements in more detail.
First, the Law had a beginning. The Law given through Moses
had not always existed; it began at a point in time. Romans
5:13,14 says, "(For until the law sin was in the world: but
sin is not imputed when there is no law. Nevertheless death
reigned from Adam to Moses, even over them that had not
sinned after the similitude of Adam's transgression, who is

170

the figure of him that was to come." We see from these verses that the Law, as given through Moses, has not always existed; there was no such Law between the time of Adam and Moses.

Galatians 3:19 says that the Law was added. But the question might be asked, To what was the Law added? The clue to the answer is found in the three preceding verses where we read about God's earlier covenant of grace made with Abraham: "Now to Abraham and his seed were the promises made. He saith not, And to seeds, as of many; but as of one, And to thy seed, which is Christ. And this I say, that the covenant, that was confirmed before of God in Christ, the law, which was four hundred and thirty years after, cannot disannul, that it should make the promise of none effect. For if the inheritance be of the law, it is no more of promise: but God gave it to Abraham by promise" (vv. 16-18).

It is important to realize that God has always dealt in grace. This was true before the Law was given, while the Law was in effect and after the Law had served its purpose. The Law did not take the place of grace, and it was not mixed with grace.

The Law was added as one railroad track is added alongside of another. Law and grace existed and worked side by side. Thus, when the Law had done its work of convicting and condemning, a person could flee to grace. It is important to remember that even during the time of the Law, salvation was by means of grace only. So it was not Law *and* grace, but Law was added to grace, or placed alongside of it.

The Law's End

Second, the Law had an end. This is actually the third element mentioned in Galatians 3:19, but we want to consider it before discussing the purpose of the Law. Galatians 3:19 says the Law was added "till the seed should come to whom the promise was made." From these words we see that there was an end to the judicial function of the Mosaic Law.

Notice the words "seed" and "promise" in the phrase "till the seed should come to whom the promise was made." What seed is being referred to? What promise is referred to?

The seed mentioned in Galatians 3:19 is specifically stated in verse 16 to be Christ—"He saith not, And to seeds, as of many; but as of one, And to thy seed, which is Christ." So we see that the Law's judicial function ended with Christ.

Another translation renders Galatians 3:19 in this way: "What then was the purpose of the Law? It was added—later on, after the promise, to disclose and expose to men their guilt—because of transgressions and [to make men more conscious of the sinfulness] of sin; and it was intended to be in effect until the Seed (the Descendant, the Heir) should come, to and concerning Whom the promise had been made" (Amplified).

In considering that the Law was in effect only until the time of Christ, notice what Galatians 4:4,5 says, "But when the fulness of the time was come, God sent forth his Son, made of a woman, made under the law, to redeem them that were under the law, that we might receive the adoption of sons."

So Jesus Christ came at the appointed time in order to fulfill the Law. Many people do not realize that the Law has been fulfilled by Jesus Christ. While He was on earth, the Lord said, "Think not that I am come to destroy the law, or the prophets: I am not come to destroy, but to fulfil. For verily I say unto you, Till heaven and earth pass, one jot or one tittle shall in no wise pass from the law, till all be fulfilled" (Matt. 5:17,18).

Jesus Christ came to earth while the Law was still in effect and lived under its jurisdiction until His death. He fulfilled the Law and thereby brought an end to its judicial function.

Another passage showing that the Law was in effect only until the time of Christ is Galatians 3:23-25: "Now before the faith came we were perpetually guarded under the Law, kept in custody in preparation for the faith that was destined to be revealed (unveiled, disclosed). So that the Law served [to us Jews] as our trainer—our guardian, our guide to Christ, to lead us—until Christ [came], that we might be justified (declared righteous, put in right standing with God) by and through faith. But now that the faith has come, we are no longer under a trainer—the guardian of our childhood" (Amplified). The Law served its purpose until Christ came, and then mankind was no longer under the judicial system of the Law.

A parallel to the change that took place after Christ came can be found in the changes made in the laws of a particular government. During special times, such as a time of war, special laws are enacted. Once the situation changes, however, people are no longer bound by those laws; they have served their purpose. Nothing is wrong with the laws themselves; they simply are no longer needed because of a new situation.

So also, nothing was wrong with the Law that God gave through Moses, but after Jesus Christ came, it was no longer necessary. Jesus Christ Himself fulfilled the Law in two ways—by keeping every jot and tittle of it and by becoming the sacrificial Lamb, slain in behalf of us who could not keep the Law.

Because Christ fulfilled the Law and brought an end to it, the Apostle Paul asked the Galatian believers, "Wherefore then serveth the law?" (3:19).

The Law's Purpose

Third, the Law had a purpose. Galatians 3:19 says the Law was added "because of transgressions." The Law was given so that sin would be revealed as a transgression. The Law showed the awfulness of sin.

Even though there was no Law from Adam to Moses, everyone had a sin nature and was guilty of sin. But something was needed to show that sin was a transgression against God. Romans 5:12,13 says, "Wherefore, as by one man sin entered into the world, and death by sin; and so death passed upon all men, for that all have sinned: (for until the law sin was in the world: but sin is not imputed when there is no law." The word "imputed" means "placed on one's account." From Adam to Moses, individual sins were not charged against a person's account because no specific law existed which showed those sins to be a transgression against God. For instance, if there were no speed limit on the highway, one could drive at any speed and not be in transgression of a specific law. But once a speed limit is set, exceeding that limit is definitely a transgression of the law.

As we consider the Old Testament times before the Mosaic Law, it is interesting to notice the situation involving Cain and Abel. Genesis 4 reveals that Cain was jealous of his brother Abel because Abel had brought a sacrifice which met the Lord's requirements. However, Cain's sacrifice was rejected (vv. 3-5). One day out in the field, Cain killed his brother (v. 8). No one apprehended Cain because at that time, there was no law against murder. This law was not enacted until Noah and his family came out of the ark after the worldwide flood (9:6).

The purpose of the Mosaic Law was to reveal to mankind in general, but to Israel in particular, the awfulness of sin in the human heart. Just as a thermometer measures temperature but does not control it, so the Law revealed sin but it did not remedy it. Or, to use another parallel, the Law served as a mirror to show man his sinful heart, but it had no ability to wash his heart clean.

The Law revealed sin and death. The Apostle Paul wrote: "For the law of the Spirit of life in Christ Jesus hath made me free from the law of sin and death. For what the law could not do, in that it was weak through the flesh, God sending his own Son in the likeness of sinful flesh, and for sin, condemned sin in the flesh" (Rom. 8:2,3).

Whereas the Law revealed sin and death, Jesus Christ revealed life. Romans 3:21,22 says, "But now the righteousness of God without the law is manifested, being witnessed by the law and the prophets; even the righteousness of God which is by faith of Jesus Christ unto all and upon all them that believe: for there is no difference."

So the Law was added, or placed alongside of, grace to reveal the sinful condition of man and to make sin a transgression against God. In addition, it allowed grace to become even more evident. "Where sin abounded, grace did much more abound" (5:20).

Sin had always been morally wrong, but under the Law it became legally wrong. Sin was made a transgression. The Law did not produce sin or make sin worse, but it was given to make sin exceedingly sinful; that is, to show the awfulness of sin. The Law revealed the true nature of sin and drove man to seek grace.

Sin has always been morally wrong, but it was not legally wrong until the Law was given. This is an important distinction, even concerning some laws today. And the opposite is also true—something may be legally right but morally wrong. For instance, gambling has been legalized in some states, but this does not make gambling right. Gambling is a moral sin. It always has been and always will be, even though it is accepted from a legal standpoint.

Also, the consumption of liquor was illegal during the prohibition period. It is now legal to drink, but this does not make it morally right. Other examples, such as abortion and divorce, could be given to support this principle. But the purpose of the Law given through Moses was to make legally wrong what was also morally wrong.

Another purpose of the Law was to convince people of sin. Romans 3:19,20 says, "Now we know that what things soever the law saith, it saith to them who are under the law: that every mouth may be stopped, and all the world may become guilty before God. Therefore by the deeds of the law there shall no flesh be justified in his sight: for by the law is the knowledge of sin."

Fallen man often thinks that he can keep the holy standards of God in his own strength. In fact, when the Law was given to the Israelites, they responded, "All that the Lord hath spoken we will do" (Ex. 19:8). They really thought they could meet God's righteous demands. But the Law demonstrated the inability of man to make himself acceptable to God. Man could not, under the moral law or any kind of law, make himself acceptable to God. This is why God provided the ceremonial law whereby man could make sacrifices for his sin.

In one sense, Israel was more blessed and pampered of God than any other nation ever has been. But even in this they provide a valuable lesson for us. God gave them the Law to prove that the best people under the most advantageous circumstances are a complete failure when it comes to keeping His holy demands.

Preparation for Christ's Coming

All of this served to prepare for the coming of the Son of God, who was proven sinless by the fact that He kept the Law perfectly and fulfilled God's righteous demands. In addition, the Lord Jesus Christ also served as God's Lamb who was slain for mankind, who had so miserably failed Him. In other words, the Lord Jesus Christ not only fulfilled the moral law, but He also completely fulfilled the ceremonial law which God had given to Israel so that they might have a way to God.

The Law did not cause sin, it only revealed sin. And the Law was in force only until Jesus Christ came and completely fulfilled it. Matthew 5:17 reveals that one of the purposes of Christ's coming was to fulfill the Law. He did not destroy it; rather, He set it aside as having any legal jurisdiction over the Church, which is His Body.

After the Lord Jesus Christ had perfectly fulfilled the Law, He ascended to the Father and sent the Holy Spirit to "reprove [convict] the world of sin, and of righteousness, and of judgment" (John 16:8). What the Law did in revealing sin is much more effectively done by the convicting power of the Holy Spirit. The Holy Spirit came on the Day of Pentecost, 50 days after the resurrection of Jesus Christ, and began His convicting work. Notice what happened. During the time of the Law, relatively few were deeply convicted of their sin, as indicated by the fact that there was only a handful of believers when Jesus Christ died, rose from the dead and went to be with the Father. But on the very first day that the Holy Spirit came, about 3000 were convicted of sin, received the message of salvation and were added to the Church (Acts 2:41,47).

It is highly significant to recognize that the Law was given specifically to Israel for a precise time—from Moses to Christ. Unless one is aware of this truth, he will not understand the present-day believer's relationship to the Law.

The Scriptures abound in passages which show that the Law was given specifically to Israel. Exodus 19:3-5 says, "And Moses went up unto God, and the Lord called unto him out of the mountain, saying, Thus shalt thou say to the house of Jacob, and tell the children of Israel; ye have seen what I did unto the Egyptians, and how I bare you on eagles' wings, and brought you unto myself. Now therefore, if ye will obey my voice indeed, and keep my covenant, then ye shall be a peculiar treasure unto me above all people: for all the earth is mine." Notice that these words were spoken to those known as "the house of Jacob" and "the children of Israel" (v. 3). The Gentile nations were not included in this special promise of blessing.

That God's agreement, or covenant, was only with the nation of Israel is also seen in Exodus 34:27: "The Lord said unto Moses, Write thou these words: for after the tenor of these words I have made a covenant with thee and with Israel." So it is clear from these references that the Law was given specifically and only to Israel.

By means of the Law, special blessings were promised to Israel and depended on Israel's obedience. This conditional element is seen in Exodus 19:5: "Now therefore, if ye will obey my voice indeed, and keep my covenant, then ye shall be a peculiar treasure unto me above all people: for all the earth is mine." However, Psalm 78 reveals how the Israelites failed to keep the Law as they wandered in the wilderness soon after they had received it. The psalmist said, "They kept not the covenant of God, and refused to walk in his law; and forgat his works, and his wonders that he had shewed them" (vv. 10,11). After telling of some of the wonderful things God had done for the people, the psalmist added, "They sinned yet more against him by provoking the most High in the wilderness. And they tempted God in their heart by asking meat for their lust. Yea, they spake against God; they said, Can God furnish a table in the wilderness?" (vv. 17-19).

Although the Mosaic covenant was conditional and the people miserably failed under it, the Abrahamic covenant was unconditional, and God will yet bless the nation in spite of individual disobedience. God will remain faithful to His promises given in the Abrahamic covenant even though the Israelites failed miserably in their responsibility under the Mosaic covenant. Even in this we see the wonderful grace of God.

Chapter 18

The Christian and the Law

Some say, "We are under the moral law but not under the ceremonial law." Others say, "We are under the moral law as a rule of life, but we are not under the Law as to salvation." That is, they are saying that we are under the Law for sanctification but not for justification. What does the Bible teach about the Christian's relationship to the Mosaic Law?

Source of Righteousness

The New Testament Books of Romans and Galatians have a great deal to say about a Christian's relationship to the Law. Romans 6:14,15 says, "For sin shall not have dominion over you: for ye are not under the law, but under grace. What then? Shall we sin, because we are not under the law, but under grace? God forbid." Galatians 5:18 says, "But if ye be led of the Spirit, ye are not under the law."

It is clear from these scriptures that the Law, as law, has absolutely nothing to contribute in accomplishing sanctification. On the contrary, being free from the bondage of the Law makes it possible for the Holy Spirit to operate effectively in the believer. A comparison of Romans 6:14,15 with Galatians 5:18 reveals that the believer is not under the Law and that he should walk in the Spirit so that he will not become entangled in the bondage of the Law. The Holy Spirit leads us on to righteousness.

Notice other scriptures that comment about the Christian's relationship to the Law. Romans 7:4 says that believers are "dead to the law." Verse 6 says they are "delivered from the law."

178

The Lord Jesus Christ not only fulfilled the Law, but He was also the end of the Law. Romans 10:3,4 says concerning Israel, "For they [Israel] being ignorant of God's righteousness, and going about to establish their own righteousness, have not submitted themselves unto the righteousness of God. For Christ is the end of the law for righteousness to every one that believeth."

Because Jesus Christ led a perfect, righteous life, He was able to fulfill the demands of the Law completely, and His righteousness was placed on our account—counted as our righteousness—when we trusted Him as personal Saviour. What glorious news! We do not become righteous by keeping the Law; we become righteous by trusting Christ as Saviour and having His righteousness placed on our account. Thus, the Apostle Paul, a Jew by birth, said that his desire was to "be found in him [Christ], not having mine own righteousness, which is of the law, but that which is through the faith of Christ, the righteousness which is of God by faith" (Phil. 3:9). The righteousness any person has in the presence of God is not that which he has produced on his own, but it is the righteousness of God that was produced in him when he trusted Jesus Christ as Saviour.

That this righteousness does not come through keeping the Law but by receiving Christ as Saviour is evident from Romans 10:10: "For with the heart man believeth unto righteousness; and with the mouth confession is made unto salvation." So the person who believes in Jesus Christ as personal Saviour is the one who becomes righteous. Every believer has this righteous standing before God. How tremendous it is to realize that the very righteousness of God is placed on our account the moment we believe Christ as Saviour. No believer can boast of such righteousness; all he can say is, "Thank You, Lord, that my standing with You is complete because of what Christ has accomplished for me."

As the believer studies the Scriptures, he learns that the Holy Spirit indwells him in order to work out His righteousness through the believer's life. This is the point of Romans 8:4: "That the righteousness of the law might be fulfilled in us, who walk not after the flesh, but after the Spirit." The indwelling Holy Spirit focuses attention on the indwelling Christ. Thus, Colossians 1:27 says, "Christ in you, the hope

of glory." That Christ lives within the believer is also seen in
Galatians 2:20: "I am crucified with Christ: nevertheless I
live; yet not I, but Christ liveth in me: and the life which I
now live in the flesh I live by the faith of the Son of God,
who loved me, and gave himself for me."

So the evidence from the Scriptures is that the Christian
is not under the Mosaic Law. Second Corinthians 3:11 refers
to the Mosaic Law as being "done away," and verse 13 refers
to it as having been "abolished." Revealing what Christ has
done to the Law, Ephesians 2:15 says, "Having abolished in
his flesh the enmity, even the law of commandments contained in ordinances." Colossians 2:14 refers to the "blotting
out" of the "handwriting of ordinances that was against us."
All this has been accomplished because Christ fulfilled every
demand of both the moral and ceremonial law.

The Law Reveals Grace

The Mosaic Law was not given to produce salvation. The
purpose of the Law was to help people see how far short they
had fallen of God's righteous demands so they would cast
themselves on the grace of God. Even during the time of the
Law grace was made available through the specified sacrifices
for sin. These pointed forward to the Lord Jesus Christ who
was the sacrifice for sin. But because Jesus Christ came and
offered Himself as the sacrifice for sin, the Law is no longer
needed.

According to Romans 5:20, the Law was given so that
God could reveal more of His grace: "Moreover the law
entered, that the offence might abound. But where sin
abounded, grace did much more abound."

When the people gathered at Mount Sinai and heard God
speak, they became frightened and "stood afar off" (Ex.
20:18). This is also the result of today's preaching of the Law
apart from the context of the grace of God.

Exodus 20:24 reveals the grace aspect of the Law, for
God instructed that an altar be made so that sacrifices, which
would bring the people into harmony with God, could be
offered.

Today, there is too much preaching of the moral law (the
Ten Commandments) without the element of grace that was

revealed in the ceremonial law. We must recognize that Jesus Christ was the sacrifice for sin and has made the grace of God available to all who will receive Him as personal Saviour.

The Christian is not under the Mosaic Law in any sense. But the whole Law is an essential part of the Scriptures, and as such it is profitable to believers of all ages. The profit of any part of the Scriptures is emphasized in II Timothy 3:16,17: "All scripture is given by inspiration of God, and is profitable for doctrine, for reproof, for correction, for instruction in righteousness: that the man of God may be perfect, throughly furnished unto all good works."

But although we are to profit from all the scriptures in that we learn valuable lessons from them, not all Scripture passages were written to us specifically. This is evident from the fact that we no longer bring sacrifices to the altar as God instructed Israel to do. Christ was our sacrifice once for all. The Bible says, "Every priest standeth daily ministering and offering oftentimes the same sacrifices, which can never take away sins: but this man, after he had offered one sacrifice for sins for ever, sat down on the right hand of God. . . . For by one offering he hath perfected for ever them that are sanctified" (Heb. 10:11,12,14). Thus, we learn from seeing the Law, in type, presenting God's righteous demands and from seeing His loving grace in the fulfillment of the Law through Christ.

Law set forth what man ought to be; grace sets forth what God is. We behold the face of Christ in the Holy Scriptures, and we see who God is by beholding Christ, "for in him dwelleth all the fulness of the Godhead bodily" (Col. 2:9). We know and understand what Christ has done for us as we study the Scriptures and see Him revealed in even the Mosaic Law. Even though the Mosaic Law is not in force for the believer today, it is important to consider what place—if any—the Law has in relationship to molding Christian character.

The Christian's Standard of Living

If the Christian is not under the Law, what is his standard of living? Basically, the standard for a Christian is to do the

will of God by the enabling grace that is supplied in Christ
Jesus our Lord through the Holy Spirit.

The key in this matter is knowing Christ. This is emphasized in II Peter 1:3: "According as his divine power hath
given unto us all things that pertain unto life and godliness,
through the knowledge of him that hath called us to glory
and virtue."

We are to have "knowledge of him," but what are we to
know about the Lord Jesus? One of the important factors we
need to know is His indwelling presence. Verse 4 says,
"Whereby are given unto us exceeding great and precious
promises: that by these ye might be partakers of the divine
nature, having escaped the corruption that is in the world
through lust." That Christ indwells the believer is also evident
from the clear statement of Colossians 1:27: "Christ in you,
the hope of glory."

Knowing about the death, burial and resurrection of
Jesus Christ is very important because these things comprise
the gospel, and unless one believes the gospel, there is no
salvation. But the Christian also needs to know that Christ
indwells him, and he needs to have an intimate relationship
with Him.

The proper formula for getting to know Christ as a
believer is presented in Romans 8:1-4: "There is therefore
now no condemnation to them which are in Christ Jesus,
who walk not after the flesh, but after the Spirit. For the law
of the Spirit of life in Christ Jesus hath made me free from
the law of sin and death. For what the law could not do, in
that it was weak through the flesh, God sending his own Son
in the likeness of sinful flesh, and for sin, condemned sin in
the flesh: that the righteousness of the law might be fulfilled
in us, who walk not after the flesh, but after the Spirit."

What a glorious truth it is to realize that "there is therefore now no condemnation to them which are in Christ
Jesus"! (v. 1). The believer's standing with God is secure.
And how wonderful it is to know that "the law of the Spirit
of life in Christ Jesus hath made me free from the law of sin
and death" (v. 2). But what is "the law of sin and death"?
This is a reference to the Law of Moses which revealed the
awfulness of sin, made sin a transgression and pronounced
death as the penalty for sin. That which has made us free

from the law of sin and death is "the law of the Spirit of life in Christ Jesus." The word "law" in this phrase is used in the sense of "principle." In other words, now that we have Jesus Christ as Saviour, we have a new life principle—"the law of the Spirit of life in Christ Jesus." Because God has set a new principle into operation within the believer, the believer is enabled to live a life of victory. Therefore, even though the believer is delivered from the Mosaic Law, the righteousness of that Law is really fulfilled in him through Christ (v. 4).

Knowing Christ Through Scripture

In order that we might know Christ, the whole body of scripture has been given to us, and, as II Timothy 3:16 indicates, it is profitable for every basic sphere of life. It is not enough to know about Christ; we must know Christ Himself.

After His resurrection the Lord Jesus appeared to two people on the way to Emmaus, and "beginning at Moses and all the prophets, he expounded unto them in all the scriptures the things concerning himself" (Luke 24:27). Later, when Jesus appeared to ten of the disciples, He told them, "These are the words which I spake unto you, while I was yet with you, that all things must be fulfilled, which were written in the law of Moses, and in the prophets, and in the psalms, concerning me" (v. 44). In this verse the Lord Jesus referred to the three major divisions of the Old Testament scriptures and emphasized that they specifically spoke of Him. So no matter what portion of the Bible we study, some aspect of the Lord Jesus Christ is being revealed to us.

Only the Scriptures "are able to make thee wise unto salvation through faith which is in Christ Jesus" (II Tim. 3:15). Only in the Holy Scriptures do we learn that Jesus Christ has paid the complete penalty for sin and that anyone who recognizes that he is a sinner and trusts Christ as personal Saviour has forgiveness of sin and eternal life. Having received Jesus Christ as Saviour, the believer is not to neglect any portion of the Scripture, because "all scripture is given by inspiration of God, and is profitable for doctrine, for reproof, for correction, for instruction in righteousness" (v. 16).

What the Scripture accomplishes in a believer's life is seen
in verse 17: "That the man of God may be perfect, throughly
furnished unto all good works." The Greek word translated
"perfect" in this verse means "complete, capable, efficient."
It is derived from a word meaning "to fit" or "to be especially adapted." The Greek word translated "throughly
furnished" has the sense of "altogether fit" or "fully fitted."
From this we see that the Scriptures lack nothing in prepar-
ing the believer to do "all good works."

The Law's Usefulness Today

In relation to the Christian, the Law has been completely
fulfilled and satisfied in Christ. It has been brought to an end
and has been done away with as a system which condemns.
However, because the Mosaic Law is part of the inspired
Scripture, it remains for all time to teach believers profitable
lessons. For instance, the moral law serves even now as a
mirror, revealing what a Christian ought to be but is not.
However, the Law cannot condemn the believer, because
Christ took the believer's condemnation when He died on the
cross. The ceremonial law serves as a type of all that Christ
has accomplished for us in that He kept the moral law
perfectly and became the sacrificial Lamb. His death in our
place made it possible for us to be free from the Law.

It is important to recognize, however, that Christ fulfilled
all aspects of the Law, and now His righteousness is imputed
to, or placed on the account of, those who receive Him as
personal Saviour. With the exception of Christ, no one has
ever been able to keep the entire Law. His ability to keep the
entire Law revealed that He was absolutely righteous; that is,
that He was God incarnate. Because He had no sin of His
own, He was able to die on the cross for our sin so that His
righteousness could be made available to all who believe.

The great mystery not known before the time of Christ
was that the perfect Christ, reflected in the entire Scriptures,
would indwell Church-Age believers. Thus, by the power of
the Holy Spirit, Jesus Christ lives His life in us.

The same person who once lived on earth and perfectly
kept the Law now lives in believers, enabling them to live the
life of victory. This is why the Scriptures make statements

such as "Christ in you, the hope of glory" (Col. 1:27) and "For ye are dead, and your life is hid with Christ in God. When Christ, who is our life, shall appear, then shall ye also appear with him in glory" (3:3,4).

Concerning what the believer has in Jesus Christ, Ephesians 4:24 says, "Put on the new man, which after God is created in righteousness and true holiness." The new man formed in every believer is Jesus Christ. Since Christ has been formed in us who have believed in Him as personal Saviour, we are to put on those things which characterize a life of righteousness and holiness. And we are to put off those things that are not honoring to Christ (v. 22). We are to say no to sin and yes to Christ. How wonderful it is to realize that the indwelling Christ gives us all the power necessary to enable us to walk as He walked. And I John 2:6 tells the believer, "He that saith he abideth in him ought himself also so to walk, even as he walked."

The Christian, because he has Christ indwelling him, has the mind of Christ available to him. Thus, the believer is to think like Christ thinks. Christians are told, "We have the mind of Christ" (I Cor. 2:16). The Bible also tells the believer, "Let this mind be in you, which was also in Christ Jesus" (Phil. 2:5). As we spend time in the whole Word of God, learning about Jesus Christ, we will think as He thinks—we will love what He loves and hate what He hates. Has the truth of the indwelling Christ really gripped your own heart? Do you recognize that He lives within you and that He is there to live out His life in you?

The Law of Christ

Believers are commanded to "fulfil the law of Christ" (Gal. 6:2). The first phrase of this verse indicates the nature of this law of Christ: "Bear ye one another's burdens." The law of Christ is really the law of love.

Jesus told His disciples, "A new commandment I give unto you, That ye love one another; as I have loved you, that ye also love one another. By this shall all men know that ye are my disciples, if ye have love one to another" (John 13:34,35). Jesus also said, "This is my commandment, That ye love one another, as I have loved you" (15:12).

Later, the Apostle John wrote: "This is his commandment, That we should believe on the name of his Son Jesus
Christ, and love one another, as he gave us commandment"
(I John 3:23). So even though a person in this age is not
bound by the Mosaic Law, there are definite commandments
of God that are in force today—"that we should believe on
the name of his Son Jesus Christ, and love one another."

The law of love is not a new law in itself because it was at
the heart of the Old Testament Law system, but to love as
Christ loved is a new law, or principle. The only reason that it
is possible for a believer to love as Christ loved is because the
believer has Christ living within him to express this love.
Thus, the Apostle Paul said, "I am crucified with Christ:
nevertheless I live; yet not I, but Christ liveth in me" (Gal.
2:20).

It is the distinct ministry of the Holy Spirit, who also
indwells the believer, to reveal the love of God through the
believer. Romans 5:5 says, "The love of God is shed abroad
in our hearts by the Holy Ghost which is given unto us." And
this love fulfills the Law. Romans 13:8,10 says, "Owe no
man any thing, but to love one another: for he that loveth
another hath fulfilled the law. . . . Love worketh no ill to his
neighbour: therefore love is the fulfilling of the law."

On the surface it may seem extremely difficult for the
believer to express this kind of love, even though the Holy
Spirit is working within him to produce this love through his
life. But the believer can have victory in this area if he will
obey the injunction of Galatians 5:16: "Walk in the Spirit,
and ye shall not fulfil the lust of the flesh." Keep in mind
that the word "walk" refers to every step we take in life.
Verse 18 assures the believer, "If ye be led of the Spirit, ye
are not under the law." As we depend on the Holy Spirit to
accomplish His ministry in us, He will give us victory over sin
and produce the love of Christ in and through our lives.

Although it is not a person's normal characteristic to love
with the kind of love Christ had, when a person receives
Christ as Saviour, He indwells his life and enables him to
express this kind of love. No wonder the Apostle Paul said, "I
can do all things through Christ which strengtheneth me"
(Phil. 4:13). What a wonderful God we have! He not only has

provided salvation for all who believe, but He has also provided victory and a loving spirit for all who will rely on Him for it.

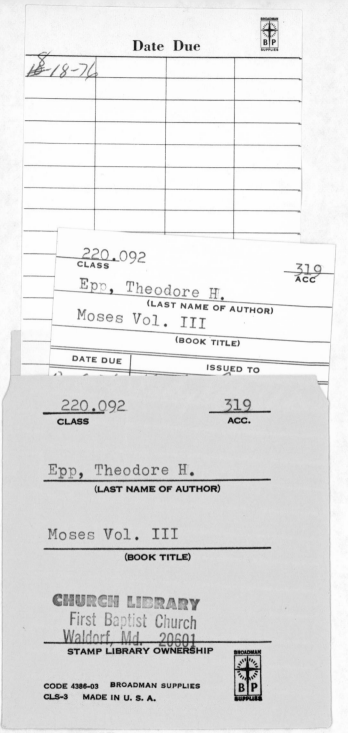